Bud E. Smith

Sams **Teach Yourself**

Google AdWords™

in **10 Minutes**

SAMS | 800 East 96th Street, Indianapolis, Indiana 46240

Associate Publisher
Greg Wiegand

Acquisitions Editor
Rick Kughen

Development Editor
Michael Henry

Managing Editor
Sandra Schroeder

Project Editor
Andy Beaster

Copy Editor
Keith Cline

Proofreader
Debbie Williams

Indexer
Erika Millen

Technical Editor
Karen Weinstein

Publishing Coordinator
Cindy Teeters

Book Designer
Anne Jones

Compositor
Gloria Schurick

Contents at a Glance

Table of Contents

About the Author

Bud Smith has written more than a dozen books about computer hardware and software, with more than a million copies sold. Bud's recent books include *Sams Teach Yourself Google Places in 10 Minutes* and *Sams Teach Yourself iPad in 10 Minutes*. He also is the author of the upcoming *Using the Apple iPad*, published by Que. Other books by Bud provide extensive coverage of Google, most recently including *How to Do Everything Nexus One, Google Business Solutions All-In-One for Dummies*, and *Google Voice for Dummies*.

Bud started out as a technical writer and journalist, and then moved into marketing and product management for technology companies. He worked at Apple Computer as a senior product manager, at Google competitor AltaVista as a group product manager, and at GPS navigation company Navman as a global product manager.

Bud holds a Bachelor of Arts degree in information systems management from the University of San Francisco and Master of Science degree in information systems from the London School of Economics. He currently lives in the San Francisco Bay Area, participating in environmental causes when he's not working on one of his many technology-related projects.

Dedication

This book is dedicated to Olga Smith and the good people at BATCS, who got my help with AdWords early on and are now taking it forward themselves.

Acknowledgments

Acquisitions editor Rick Kughen led the charge for this much-needed book about AdWords, a new and important service for business. Project editor Andrew Beaster and development editor Michael Henry improved my syntax and shortened sentences that needed it. Technical editor Karen Weinstein and copy editor Keith Cline checked all the steps and instructions to help make them clear and correct.

We Want to Hear from You!

As the reader of this book, *you* are our most important critic and commentator. We value your opinion and want to know what we're doing right, what we could do better, what areas you'd like to see us publish in, and any other words of wisdom you're willing to pass our way.

You can email or write me directly to let me know what you did or didn't like about this book—as well as what we can do to make our books stronger.

Please note that I cannot help you with technical problems related to the topic of this book, and that due to the high volume of mail I receive, I might not be able to reply to every message.

When you write, please be sure to include this book's title and author as well as your name and phone or email address. I will carefully review your comments and share them with the author and editors who worked on the book.

E-mail: consumer@samspublishing.com

Mail: Greg Wiegand
Associate Publisher
Sams Publishing
800 East 96th Street
Indianapolis, IN 46240 USA

Reader Services

Visit our website and register this book at informit.com/register for convenient access to any updates, downloads, or errata that might be available for this book.

Introduction

Google AdWords is a huge opportunity for businesses and other organizations to improve their results from Google search, to increase sales, to try out new business ideas, and in general to make the Web friendlier. However, it's also a way to spend money without realizing much return. Helping you to use AdWords effectively from day one—and, just as important, from dollar one—is the goal of this book.

AdWords can get you in front of customers who you could never have reached otherwise. If they enter a search term that you've successfully bid on, they see your ad. You can choose to selectively run your ad only in certain geographic locations, and only at certain times of day, pointing the user to any web page destination you want. You can start and stop an AdWords campaign whenever you like.

What's more, AdWords is pay-per-click advertising. You can have literally thousands of people see your AdWords ad and get your messaging—and perhaps, thereby, become that much more ready to buy from you in the future. Yet you pay for the ad only when someone clicks it. And that click gives you a chance to convert the web user into a paying customer.

The difficult part is making sure to get the most out of all this. AdWords is a highly competitive marketplace. There are people out there who are very good at converting clicks into cash. You need to be able to match or exceed them from the very beginning.

Luckily, you are the only one in the world with your unique business idea, service, support, place (or places) of business, and other distinguishing characteristics. Using AdWords can help you identify and take advantage of your unique qualities, improving not only your AdWords performance, but everything about your business.

This book, although small, covers the whole spectrum—from the mechanics of setting up an AdWords ad, to using AdWords reporting to see how your ad is performing, to making AdWords work for you and your business or organization. And it does so in short, focused, 10-minute lessons that you can absorb easily and put to work immediately.

You can get a quick hit of benefits from AdWords without much work. Simply do what many of the "big boys" do and create an AdWords ad tied to your business name, and any common variations on it or misspellings of it that people might use instead.

You can include your own name and variations on it, if people strongly associate you with your business. You can also include product or service names that people associate with your business. Use geographic targeting to run the AdWords ad such that it appears in whatever geographic locations *your* customers live, work, and search online.

Then, when people search for your business, or for you, AdWords helps ensure that they get where they're going. This simple strategy alone can make your investment of time and money in AdWords worthwhile.

To take AdWords further, beyond these useful basic steps, requires thinking through several important areas; each requires a certain degree of mastery to do well. Luckily, this book is here to help. These key areas are as follows:

▶ **Keyword tie-ins.** What keywords do you want to "own," making sure that any qualified Google users see your ad when they enter that specific keyword?

▶ **Ad text.** What can you say, in about 10 or 12 words, that's more or less certain to get a potential customer to click your ad? How can you make sure the right people click and the wrong people don't?

▶ **Landing pages.** When users do click your ad, they can go to any web page you specify. What can you do on that landing page to most effectively convince your web visitors to become paying customers?

▶ **Geographic targeting.** What are the geographic areas your ad must show up in for your natural customers to see what you have available? What areas are "nice to haves," where your ad showing up is good as long as it's not too expensive?

▶ **Reporting.** How can you get the most out of the powerful, but somewhat limited, AdWords reporting tools? At what point will you need to consider moving to Google's free, powerful, but potentially confusing Google Analytics tool?

▶ **Managing costs.** What's a reasonable amount to spend on Google AdWords advertising? And how do you measure your return to be sure that you're getting your money's worth?

▶ **Websites and social media.** At the end of the day, both AdWords and social media are largely devices for bringing people to your website. How can you improve your site so that it helps you convert customers' interest in you into cold, hard cash?

Business is always complicated, but AdWords brings in a whole new set of buzzwords and skills to master. Its presence gives either you, or your competitors, a way to get more business, more of the time, with less effort (less effort, that is, after the initial setup is done).

So, let it be you who benefits. This book, and the easy-to-use tools that Google has pulled together into its AdWords offering, will be like a magic carpet, taking you to places you never dreamed of going before. You can create a thriving online business, whether it's standalone or a complement to a real-world, perhaps bricks-and-mortar, presence.

About This Book

As part of the *Sams Teach Yourself in 10 Minutes* guides, this book aims to teach you the ins and outs of using Google AdWords without using up a lot of precious time. Divided into easy-to-follow lessons that you can tackle in about 10 minutes each, you learn the following AdWords tasks and topics:

▶ Creating an AdWords account

▶ Writing your first AdWords ad

▶ Identifying your target markets, demographically and geographically

▶ Deciding where you want your ads to appear

▶ Setting your budget and creating an approach to bidding

▶ Identifying the keywords that will bring customers to you

▶ Writing great ads that appeal to your target markets

- ▶ Starting and expanding your ad campaign
- ▶ Using day-of-week and time-of-day ad targeting
- ▶ Using AdWords tools to improve your results
- ▶ Using AdWords reports to improve your return on investment
- ▶ Improving your website for better AdWords results
- ▶ Moving up to Google Analytics

After you finish these lessons, and the others in this book, you'll know all you need to know to take Google AdWords as far as you want it to go.

Who This Book Is For

This book is aimed at all business owners, or leaders of other kinds of organizations, who want to create a Google AdWords account and use AdWords to attract customers or clients online. This should mean just about everyone! You might have extensive computer and online experience or you might have very little. You might also have some experience in marketing your business or organization through various means, including print and/or online media, or you might have very little marketing background.

Throughout this book, the term *business owners* is meant very broadly. If you work in a social services agency, a public facility such as a swimming pool, or a nonprofit, you have people who you might call *clients*, *customers*, or some other term. They still need to know about what you're offering and how to take advantage of it. So, *business* means any store, location, or service provider that's open to the public!

Each lesson in this book focuses on one specific topic, such as creating your Google AdWords account or identifying keywords that your customers consider relevant. You can skip from one topic to another, read the book through from start to finish, or both. You can hand it to friends, family members, or colleagues to answer a specific question that they have, too.

What Do I Need to Use This Book?

You will need a computer with a web browser and reliable Internet access to use this book. A tablet computer, such as the iPad, or a small, low-cost netbook will probably not be adequate for the tasks needed; you will probably want either a Windows PC or a Macintosh. Either a desktop or a laptop model will do the job.

If you are not experienced with computers, or don't have a computer, you might want to buy a computer and procure Internet access, and then learn how to use the computer itself and a web browser before proceeding.

Alternatively, you can find a friend or work colleague with the necessary equipment and skills, and get that person's help in carrying out the tasks involved. If you are the one with the necessities, you can provide help to others; it's fun to work together on tasks such as those involved with a Google AdWords presence.

Conventions Used in This Book

Whenever you need to push a particular button on your computer or click a particular control onscreen, you'll find the label or name for that item bolded in the text, such as "click the **Home** button." In addition to the text and figures in this book, you'll also encounter some special boxes labeled Tip, Note, or Caution.

> TIP: Tips offer helpful shortcuts or easier ways to do something.

> NOTE: Notes are extra bits of information related to the text that might help you expand your knowledge or understanding.

> CAUTION: Cautions are warnings or other important information you need to know about the consequences of using a feature or executing a task

PLAIN ENGLISH: Not sure what a term means? Read these to expand your geek vocabulary and get a better handle on [insert topic here].

Screen Captures

The graphics captured for this book come from a Windows PC running Internet Explorer 8 and showing various web pages, mostly in Google AdWords. You might use a Macintosh, or you might use a Windows PC running a different version of Windows.

You might use a different web browser, or a different version of Internet Explorer, and different settings for your computer and your web browser. For any of these reasons, your screens might look somewhat different from those in the book. Also keep in mind that the developers of Google AdWords and the software and other websites shown in this book are constantly working to improve their software, websites, and the services offered on them.

New features are added regularly to the Windows and Mac OS, software, and websites, and old ones change or disappear. This means that screen content changes often, so your own screens might differ from the ones shown in this book. Don't be too alarmed, however. The basics, although they are tweaked in appearance from time to time, stay mostly the same in principle and usage.

LESSON 1

Getting More Business with AdWords

In this lesson, you learn just what an AdWords ad is and how it works for users. You then start your journey behind the scenes to understand how an advertiser creates an AdWords ad, how it's paid for, and some of the finer points of making your ads effective—as well as how AdWords and search engine optimization (SEO) work together.

Identifying AdWords Ads

Google AdWords is one of the greatest success stories of our time. Just as TV advertising revolutionized television and made it a huge cultural force, for better or worse, so Google AdWords has revolutionized the use of the Internet.

AdWords has made the Internet highly profitable, both for Google and for many AdWords advertisers. The success of AdWords has also encouraged others to find ways of making money from the Internet that aren't much like AdWords at all.

Google has recently introduced a new feature, Google Instant. With Google Instant, Google uses *predictive search*—that is, it guesses what the user is going to enter, based on whatever characters he's already typed. This tends to steer users toward popular results.

> **PLAIN ENGLISH: Google Instant**
>
> Google Instant is a predictive search capability that makes search faster by guessing what the users are going to enter as their search query. It's turned on by default in Google Search, but users can turn it off. (From the main Google search page, click **Settings->Search Settings**. Choose the radio button, **Do Not Use Google Instant**, and click **Save Preferences**.) Early indications, though, are that most users like it and will leave it turned on.

Figure 1.1 shows a Google search results page in mid-search, with Google Instant running. The page has four different kinds of search results:

- ▶ **Google Instant hints.** Google's recently introduced search feature, Google Instant, offers the user hints to common searches that are related to whatever characters the user has typed so far. The user can then choose the rest of the search from the dropdown list of hints or keep typing. These hints can steer the search away from what users might have come up with on their own, and they take up valuable screen real estate.

- ▶ **AdWords results.** These are the new kind of search results—originally found only out of the way, on the right side of the page, but now often found above the organic listings as well, although clearly marked. Note how the only AdWords ad shown, while Google Instant is working, is for the first term in Google Instant's list of choices.

- ▶ **Organic search results.** These are the original kind of search results, determined purely by Google's algorithms, with no money changing hands. These pure listings are called *organic* search results. (Although this is an organic crop that's often fertilized by money, in the form of investment in search engine optimization, or SEO, by companies that appear in the results.)

> **PLAIN ENGLISH: Organic Search Results**
>
> *Organic search results* are the original kind of search results, the ones determined by search engine algorithms, with no money changing hands. The term is used to distinguish these pure search results from AdWords ads, local search results, and other kinds of search results displayed alongside the organic results.

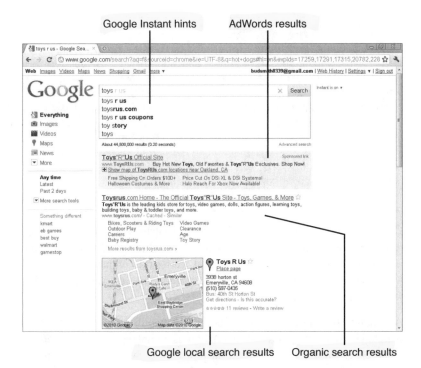

FIGURE 1.1   Google Maps makes local business searches easy.

▶ **Local search results.** When a search term seems to represent
  something that's available to buy locally, Google provides local
  results. Business locations are shown placed on a map, with some
  results highlighted versus others.

> PLAIN ENGLISH: **Local Search**
>
> *Local search* is search that's influenced by the location of the user. The search engine guesses the user's location by various technical means, and then uses the location as a central point for a local search. The search engine also typically enables the user to change the assumed location, in case it's wrong. (Which is also useful if the user is currently at work, perhaps, in San Francisco, but wants to search near his home across the bay in, say, Oakland.) Both local and global search are useful for different purposes; for instance, you might search for *cashews* to learn about cashew production worldwide—or you might just want to step out of your office and buy some cashews.

Companies use AdWords to complement or bolster the search engine results they get from organic search. You'll often find, when you search on a company name, that there's an AdWords ad for the company at the top of the search results—and that the very next entry is an organic search result for the same company.

An example of duplicate entries—one from AdWords, one from organic search—is shown in Figure 1.1. An AdWords ad linking to the Toys "R" Us website, ToysRUs.com, is positioned just above the top organic search result, which links to the same company. If you click the AdWords ad, it costs the company money, but it wants the click so badly that it's willing to pay for it if needed.

Figure 1.2 shows the same search when the user finishes his search by pressing the Return key after entering just the word *toys*. Many more AdWords ads appear, and there are three organic search results, not just one. However, ToysRUs is still the leading organic search result and the second AdWords result.

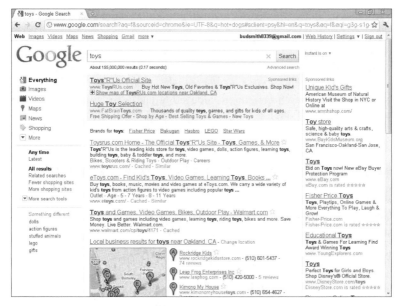

FIGURE 1.2 You can find AdWords ads and organic search results together.

TIP: **Print and Save AdWords Pages**

AdWords can seem overwhelming, with its many options, definitions, and of course expenses. Google offers a lot of options in AdWords and a great deal of information online, but you might have trouble finding it again when you need it. You might want to consider printing out key information and screenshots from your browser and putting them in a binder. Of course, the contents of your AdWords site change over time, and help information and so on gets updated as well. So, set up the print options in your browser to include the URL of the current web page in the printout so that you can return to the same page again and see the most recent information when you need to.

NOTE: **Fewer Organic Search Results Above the Fold**

Because users don't like to scroll, the area "above the fold"—that is, in the first screenful of results that users see, without scrolling—is vital. This area is now dominated by AdWords ads at the top and side, and local results, where applicable, at the bottom. Organic search results are reduced to just a few entries (sometimes only one).

How AdWords Works for Users

What does Google AdWords do for users? Basically, it gives them choices. Google's organic search results are good (which is why Google is the top search engine), but they have their problems.

Websites that have been around for a long time, and are referred to by other older sites, get a lot of respect—that is, high search engine rankings—from Google. It's difficult for something new, exciting, and potentially lucrative to quickly earn a strong position in organic search results. (Although there are a lot of SEO practitioners out there trying to help their clients do just that.)

For users who are of a mind to buy something, the AdWords ads that appear alongside their search results are often more interesting, and more valuable, than the organic search results. The AdWords results are lively and action oriented. They don't relate to what is or isn't a valuable information resource; they relate to helping you get a product or service that will help you fill a need of some sort or get something done.

An old IBM ad sums this up well. A couple of consultants tell a CEO a great plan for turning his business around. The CEO tells the consultants to make it happen. One consultant looks at the other and says, horrified: "He wants us to *do* something?" The advice-givers then leave, shaking their heads in disgust at the idea of actually being responsible for making something happen. Organic search results can be like these consultants who just want to tell you information.

AdWords ads help users do something. As a creator of AdWords ads, you will benefit by keeping the user's perspective in mind. You don't need to trick or mislead users into clicking your AdWords ad; often, the user wants to find an ad to click. You just need to make your ad promising in relation to what the user wants to accomplish at that moment, and to the kind of product or service that will help her do that.

Look at the AdWords ads in Figure 1.2. They're action oriented. Your ad should be similar.

How AdWords Works for Sellers

AdWords ads seem simple from a user's point of view. However, from the vendor's point of view, there's a fundamental principle and a few wrinkles that you should be aware of.

The fundamental principle is that you focus on keywords. Let's say that you have a raft of hot dog stands in Chicago called Frank's Fast Franks. You want your AdWords ad to appear anytime someone in Chicago enters certain keywords (which can be a phrase or just individual words). Here's a list of keywords that might apply, from most specific to least specific:

- ▶ Frank's Fast Franks
- ▶ Frank's
- ▶ Franks
- ▶ Hot dog stand
- ▶ Hot dogs
- ▶ Hot dogs lunch
- ▶ Frankfurter
- ▶ Sauerkraut
- ▶ Chili dog
- ▶ Cheap lunch

You can imagine that a lot of people are competing for these keywords, because there's money involved—lunch money. (Chicago has about three million people, so if each of them were to spend $10 on lunch, that would be $30 million up for grabs every day at lunchtime.)

When you do search engine optimization for organic search for your website, you're competing for placement with everyone in the world who might want to sell hot dogs (or who might be named Frank) and who might want to get their share of that $30 million or so of Chicago lunch money.

You might guess that, as a local hot dog vendor, you would probably lose out, in terms of search engine placement, to companies that sell hot dogs in supermarkets or national hot dog chains. (Google local search is slowly changing this situation, but that's still a work in progress. See my book *Teach Yourself Google Places in 10 Minutes* for more about Google local search and how to win there, as well.)

Figure 1.3 shows actual search results for *hot dogs* for a search made from Oakland, California. Note that the top organic search result is from Wikipedia. This is increasingly common as Wikipedia gets linked to from more and more sites that want to offer a definition or background material relating to a term. Wikipedia is a great example of a search result that scores high for being informative and low for enabling the searcher to actually do anything, such as buy and eat a hot dog for lunch right away.

FIGURE 1.3   Wikipedia is top dog for hot dogs.

As an AdWords vendor, you bid on a keyword, such as *hot dogs*. You might agree to pay, say, up to 10 cents every time someone clicks your ad that shows up when a Google user enters *hot dogs* as a search term.

CAUTION: **Bidder Beware**
The amount you need to bid on a keyword to get your ad to appear varies based on many different factors. See Lesson 11, "Finding Your Keywords," for more details.

One great thing about AdWords is that you can just bid locally. With local bidding, you don't need to beat every AdWords vendor around the world interested in promoting their hot dogs or related products. You just need to beat the ones in, say, Chicago. You can place your AdWords ad in Chicago only or even in specific areas of Chicago. (You'll have to try geographic targeting in your area, as described in Lesson 6, "Deciding Where to Show Your Ads," to find out just how fine-tuned Google enables you to get in your local area.)

Finer Points of AdWords for Sellers

You probably understand now, if you didn't before, the basic process with AdWords: You bid on specific keywords (which includes phrases as well as individual words), and if you bid enough, your ad shows up on search results pages. There are some fine points of this, though, that are worth mentioning, to help you be more effective with your use of AdWords. Three main points stand out.

The first point is that Google was the first major vendor of online ad inventory to commit strongly to what is called *pay-per-click advertising*. Other vendors wanted to charge you every time your ad was *shown*. Google committed to charging advertisers only when the user *clicks* the ad.

Pay per click is great for advertisers. It means that a lot of the risk for you is removed. You get lots of free brand-building with users who see your ad, and perhaps even read it fairly closely, but don't click. Google puts your ad onscreen all those times without getting paid. You only have to pay when the user does click your ad. You can get a lot of exposure without paying too much money. When you do pay, it's only when you've at least gotten the user to do something.

However, this leads to the second major point, which is the placement of your ad. Google AdWords advertisers are endlessly confused that they don't get the top AdWords position simply by paying the most for a specific keyword. (Often, Google will put its top one, two, or three AdWords ads above the organic search results, as shown in Figure 1.1. This kind of placement is golden for the AdWords advertiser, and advertisers are willing to pay highly for ads that appear there and get clicked.)

However, Google puts your ad on top of the AdWords list only if you have a fairly high bid on your keyword *and* lots of people click your ad. That's because Google wants to make money, and it makes more money from 1,000 clicks at just 10 cents a click—that is, $100—than it does from 100 clicks at 20 cents a click, which is $20. So, your ad placement is a combination of something you do control—your keyword bid—and something you don't directly control, which is how many people click your ad.

The final point is something that marketing experts have been aware of for a long time but that you're going to learn now in a way that's very specific to your business: conversion. It's not worth paying for people to click your ad if you don't make money from at least some of the clickers over time.

Figure 1.4 is a conceptual diagram of the conversion process. It's like a funnel. Here are the steps in the funnel, with some made-up numbers as an example:

- ▶ 1,000 people see your AdWords ad.

- ▶ 5% of the people who see it, or 50 people, click it (which costs you $5 total, if you pay 10 cents per click).

- ▶ 50 people thereby see your landing page, which tells them where they can get a hot dog from you.

- ▶ 10 people actually go to get a hot dog from you.

- ▶ You make $1 profit per customer, so you make $10.

Now you've just spent $5 for the clicks and made $10 in immediate profit. This is a pretty good investment, especially if some of the clickers keep coming back for your hot dogs over time, increasing your profit from the ad.

However, it's a lot of overhead and hassle to know, or at least guess, just how much profit you made from a direct result of your AdWords ad. My own observation is that AdWords is now popular enough that most of the easy money is gone. You aren't likely to sell 1,000 hot dogs by paying $10 for AdWords ads. Results that are more like the example given—you double your investment in the short term, and get additional benefits from repeat sales over time—is a more realistic target for your AdWords advertising efforts.

What this means, though, is that fairly close tracking of the results of your AdWords spending is important. You need to at least be able to quickly separate your AdWords efforts into three groups: clearly profitable; borderline profitable, depending on the long-term impact; and clearly unprofitable. If you don't have a firm enough grasp of your conversion process to at least be able to make this kind of distinction, it can be quite easy to waste money on AdWords and not even know that you're losing money as you go along.

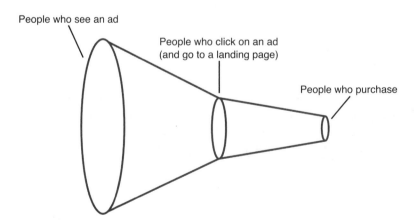

People who see an ad

People who click on an ad
(and go to a landing page)

People who purchase

FIGURE 1.4   Conversion is crucial to sales—and to AdWords.

CAUTION: **Watch Profits, Not Revenues**

Many small businesspeople confuse revenues and profits. For instance, they might think an ad campaign (or AdWords effort) pays off if it costs them $20 and they get $100 in sales in return. This might be true, but only if that $100 in sales gets them at least $20 in immediate profit, before the ad cost. If the $100 in sales comes mostly from low-margin items, or even from loss-leader items that lose money, that $20 advertising cost might not be repaid by $100 in sales at all.

Search Engine Optimization and AdWords

You are likely to be hearing a lot about search engine optimization (SEO), which refers to trying to get high search engine rankings for your website on the keywords that best fit your areas of interest. Some SEO techniques border on the illegitimate, such as creating little webs of more or less fake sites to pump up the number of people following links to your real site. Perhaps you're wondering how SEO affects your AdWords effort.

AdWords is an effective and legitimate quick fix for SEO problems. You might have a new outboard motor to sell in the United States that's perfect for boats used for waterskiing. AdWords is an obvious shortcut for getting a link to your website in front of key audiences in the specific geographic areas you care about.

Also, the things you learn from creating and deploying your AdWords ads are applicable to your SEO work for your website. Your work on your AdWords ads will show you which keywords are most hotly contested, what gets users to click, and more. This will inform your SEO work for your website.

Conversely, the results from your SEO work can also go into your AdWords efforts. Each can complement the other. One trick is to identify odd, but powerful, keywords and use them across all your effort.

For instance, one business that I helped sells a book and training sessions about reducing your foreign accent when speaking English (see Figure 1.5). Of the many keywords that are possible for this business, one powerful one turned out to be *elocution*. (Perhaps influenced by the musical *My Fair Lady*, about a lower-class girl who becomes a hit socially largely by mastering an upper-class English accent.) *Elocution* worked first on AdWords, but now it's about to be integrated into the main site, as well.

> TIP: **Consider AdWords Alongside SEO**
>
> AdWords and SEO complement each other. Of the two, AdWords is more straightforward and its results are easier to track. AdWords is also a good way to test SEO strategies before you implement them on your website. Don't spend money on SEO without also considering whether you can get similar or better results through AdWords. If you hire an SEO consultant, consider searching for one who also knows how to use AdWords effectively.

FIGURE 1.5   Elocution is great if you're BaTCS.

FIGURE 2.1 A Google account opens the door to many services.

▶ **Gmail.** Google's popular online email program. Gmail accounts are very flexible for sending and receiving all kinds of email, and you get many gigabytes of online email storage for free.

▶ **Talk.** Google Talk is an instant messenger service that's well integrated with Gmail.

▶ **Calendar.** Google's online calendaring program is also quite flexible. You can use and share access among various calendars at once—for instance, you can have a personal calendar that only you can access, alongside flexible calendars for a team you play on, a group you belong to, and more.

▶ **Docs.** Google Docs gives you easy-to-use, simpler versions of Microsoft Word (word processing program), Excel (spreadsheet program), and PowerPoint (presentation program). Again, your files are very easily shared, and they can be edited by several people at one time.

▶ **Sites.** Sites is a service for creating and maintaining a free website, but unfortunately, it's more oriented toward intranet sites (a site used within a company) than toward true websites used by the general public.

▶ **Voice.** Google Voice gives you a single, virtual phone number that you can use with your mobile phone, home phone, and more. It's a bit complicated, but very powerful.

▶ **Blogger.** Blogger is probably the easiest service around for creating and maintaining a blog, which can be a great way to communicate with customers as well as friends, family, and people who share your interests. (To cover all these bases effectively, you might need several blogs.)

▶ **YouTube.** You can use YouTube without an account, but with one, you can store preferences and upload videos of your own. This includes videos that you then display on your website.

▶ **Groups.** Groups is an email subscription list and an online repository for files—all good things for a business to have.

Google has dozens of additional offerings—some of which do more for you if you have a Google account, others of which don't. (Google search, for instance, works pretty much the same way whether or not you have a Google account.)

One of the most important Google services, which Google doesn't present separately, is Google Contacts. Contacts is a database of people that you are in, well, contact with. It's quite powerful and flexible, especially when you use it with multiple other Google services such as Gmail, Calendar, Docs, and Google Voice.

Among Google's many services, AdWords is a bit unusual in that it requires you to have a separate account. You still use your Google account sign-in to access AdWords, but you create your AdWords account separately, and you can also delete it without affecting your main Google account.

Creating a Business Google Account

The comedian Steve Martin once made a funny joke about the martial arts movie *Crouching Tiger, Hidden Dragon*. He said that he was disappointed not to see any tigers or dragons in it—until he realized that they were actually present, but "the tigers were crouching, and the dragons were hidden."

Creating a Google account is a bit similar to the movie. It's very easy to create a Google account using an existing email account, and never get involved with Gmail (Google's web-based email program) at all. However, the somewhat hidden way to create a Google account—by creating a Gmail account first—is the better option.

Why? First, having a Gmail account is pretty cool. Gmail is extremely flexible, and very easy to use as a kind of giveaway email address. You can easily take email sent to your Gmail account and forward it to some other email account, block it, or assign a label to it. You can even ask Gmail to go get your email from some other account, deliver it to you, and label your replies as if they came from the other account.

The other cool thing about Gmail is that Gmail accounts, like diamonds, are forever. A Gmail account is not dependent on a specific employer, Internet service provider, or anything else that's likely to change. Gmail is also famous for providing almost unlimited storage, so you're unlikely to overfill your inbox (or to have to manage its size as you go along). Plus, being so flexible, Gmail doesn't force itself on you—you can use it alongside one or more other accounts with no problem.

All this means that a Gmail account is a useful thing to have, as well as being the best choice for your default email account to use with your

Google account. As you create a Gmail account, I recommend that you take the option that's offered to also create a Google account, with your Gmail account as its entry point. That way, part of your digital world is all Google, all the time.

If your business is of any size at all—or, if you hope that it will be some-day—consider creating a separate Gmail account and Google account for your business. Google itself recommends this. That way, you can give business partners and employees access, allow other people to cover while you're on vacation, and even perhaps someday transfer the account when you sell your business, all without interfering with your personal email and other personal or separate business activities.

You should also consider using a business-friendly name for your Gmail account, such as happypizza@gmail.com instead of an account based on your personal name. Using a business-friendly account name promotes a pro-fessional appearance, usability by multiple individuals, and transferability.

TIP: **Do You Need to Use a Domain Name?**

The domain name is the second part of an email address—the part after the @ symbol. It also shows up in your website address; google.com is a domain name. It's long been considered the ultimate in professionalism to have your business's domain name as part of your email address—for instance, joe.bloggs@happypizza.com. Using a different domain name, as in happypizza@gmail.com, was considered amateurish. However, more and more people, even in big companies, are using Gmail and other third-party email addresses for work purposes. You can still create an email address that uses you business domain name and autoforward it to your Gmail address if you prefer, but it's probably okay to just use the Gmail address directly.

You can also move staffers to Google services. It reduces your training and support costs and investment of time if you have everyone on the same services and makes working together easier. For instance, if you're all on Google Calendar, you can more easily share calendars. You might, howev-er, want to give staffers a work-specific Google account so that their per-sonal information doesn't get mixed up with work information. (You might not really want to know just how often a colleague is going in for a pedicure.)

> NOTE: **Consider Using Google Apps**
>
> Google Apps is a paid service from Google that, at this writing, costs $50 per user per year. The home page for Google Apps is shown in Figure 2.2. Google Apps is used by many businesses and organizations, including government agencies. It can be tied into your company's domain name and includes additional Gmail storage, Google Docs storage, the ability to turn off text ads in Google services, guaranteed uptime, better security, and improved customer support.

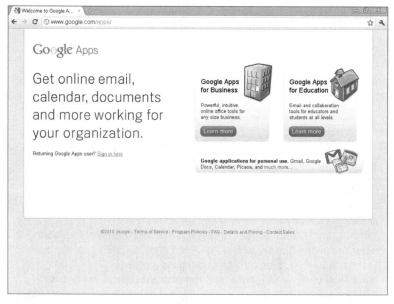

FIGURE 2.2   Google Apps is a powerful choice for businesses.

PLAIN ENGLISH: **Service Level Agreement**

A service level agreement (SLA) is a document that commits a service provider to certain specific benchmarks, such as providing website uptime of 99.8%, which would mean the site could only be down 17 hours a year or less. Although this seems like a steep commitment, it does allow the site owners a bit of room for software upgrades, site maintenance, unexpected downtimes, and so on. Google Apps provides an SLA with an uptime guarantee of 99.9% as part of its service, and you should consider asking for SLAs from your other service providers (and providing them to your customers, if doing so makes sense in your business).

Signing Up for Your Gmail and Google Account

If you already have a Google account for your business, you can skip this section and go to the section "Setting Up Your AdWords Account," later in this lesson.

Follow these steps to set up a Gmail account, which is the easiest and most powerful way to create a Google account:

NOTE: **Creating an AdWords Account Directly**

If you are certain that you want to begin by using AdWords only, and not Gmail or other Google services, you can begin the process of creating a Google account by going to http://www.adwords.com. The steps will be similar to those described here. However, I recommend that you create a new Gmail account, specifically for your business, as described here.

1. Go to the Gmail home page at http://www.gmail.com.

   If you are not already signed in to a Gmail account, the Welcome to Gmail page appears. If you are already signed in to a Google account, your user identifier appears in the upper-right corner of the web page, along with a Sign Out link. If the Google account you are logged in to includes the use of Gmail, your Gmail inbox will appear.

2. If you are already signed in to a Google account, click the Sign Out link.

The Gmail home page appears.

3. Click the **Create an Account** button.

The Create a Google Account - Gmail page appears, as shown in Figure 2.3.

4. Enter your first and last name.

You can use your personal name—you can always change this later—or a generic name that describes your role, such as Store Manager.

5. Enter your desired login name, and then click the **Check Availability** button. Keep trying until you find a name that's suitable for your business and available.

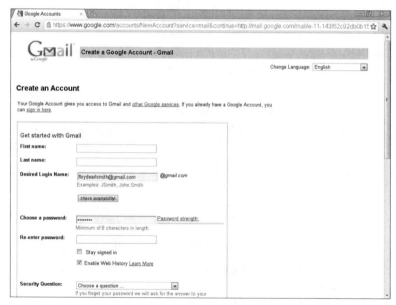

FIGURE 2.3   Create your Google account through Gmail.

This can be tricky because you can't use a name that's already in use as a Google account name. Use a name that's as close to your business name as possible. If the name you want is chosen, consider adding your town or city name—and shortening the other parts of the name if needed.

If you can't find a name you like a lot right off the bat, stop the process, consider alternatives, and discuss your options with people you trust. If you really get stuck, you can use a non-Gmail email address to create your Google account. In that case, start the preceding process at http://www.google.com, not http://www.gmail.com, and skip the login name step.

6. Choose a password.

   Keep your password stored someplace safe because it's an important asset of your business, and change it periodically, including whenever an employee who might have known the password leaves the business.

7. Enter the necessary information in the remaining fields.

   Be sure to enter a recovery email address as a backup—but be aware that anyone currently involved in the business could move on, including you, so don't count on the recovery email address too much.

8. Review the terms of service, and then click the **I Accept. Create My Account** button.

   Your account is created.

TIP: **Make Sure Your Name is Right**

After you set up your account, ask around and make sure that the account name you chose is a good one. If it's not, create a new account with the name you want, and then delete the old one. To do this, sign in at the http://www.google.com/accounts/login page. Next to the My Products list, click the **Edit** link, and from there you can delete your account.

You can use your Gmail account for a wide variety of purposes—more than just about any other kind of email account. You can use your Gmail account to retrieve email from your other accounts, to send email in the guise of other accounts, and more.

Your Gmail account is very powerful and flexible. To get the most out of it, ask a friend or colleague who has experience with Gmail, or find a suitable book, such as *Sams Teach Yourself Gmail in 10 Minutes* by Steve Holzner (Sams, 2010). Also, sign in to Gmail and click the **Help** link to learn more.

Signing Up for Your AdWords Account

After you've signed up for a Google account via Gmail, you can take the additional step of signing up for your AdWords account. Follow these steps:

1. Go to the Google home page at http://www.google.com.

   The Google home page appears.

2. Choose **Settings**, **Google Account Settings**.

   Your Google Accounts page appears, as shown in Figure 2.4.

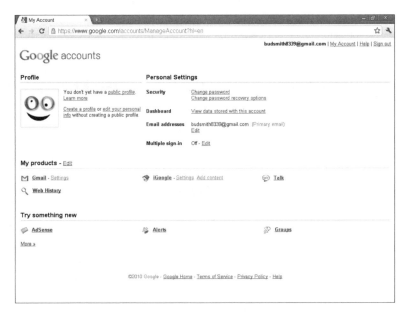

FIGURE 2.4   Google Accounts shows the Google services you've already signed up for—and offers you more.

3. Look under the Try Something New header. If a link for AdWords appears, click the **AdWords** link. If not, click the **More** link, find the AdWords link, and then click the **AdWords** link.

   The AdWords sign-in page appears, as shown in Figure 2.5.

4. Take the time to explore the Google AdWords sign-in page, including the things AdWords can do for you (under Learn About AdWords) and business solutions that work with AdWords (under Related Programs).

   There is a great deal of information linked to from the Google AdWords sign-in page, some of which might be directly applicable to you, now or in the future.

5. Enter your Google password and click the **Sign In** button.

Your Google AdWords account is created and you are taken to the setup page. Set your time zone and currency preferences, as shown in Figure 2.6.

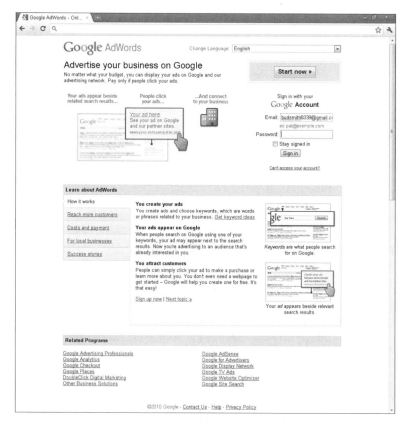

FIGURE 2.5   The Google AdWords sign-in page shows what AdWords does.

CAUTION: You Can Only Set These Preferences Once

You can set your time zone and currency preferences only once. If you want to change them later, you have to delete the account, and then create a new AdWords account. This can be frustrating. I once made an international move from the United Kingdom to the United States, and had to start all over in AdWords. However, it's an important security precaution.

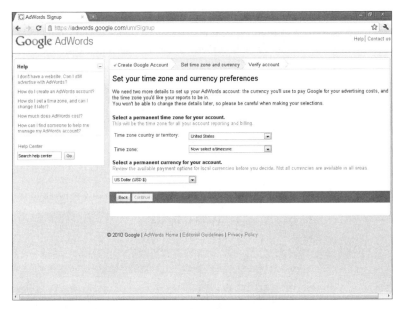

FIGURE 2.6   Set your time zone and currency carefully.

6. Choose your time zone country or territory from the pull-down menu.

   A message appears onscreen: "Your time zone and currency settings can't be changed after you setup your account. Please review your choices carefully and then click 'Continue.'" Choose carefully because this is a one-time deal for this AdWords account.

7. If needed, choose your time zone from the pull-down menu.

   If the country you choose has multiple time zones, choose the one that's appropriate for you from the pull-down menu.

8. Choose the currency for the account.

   You are asked to choose from a long list, even if the country you choose only has one currency, as most do.

9. Click the **Continue** button.

A message confirms that your AdWords account has been created, as shown in Figure 2.7. It also tells you that you can't run any ads until you enter a billing method. How to do this is described in the next lesson.

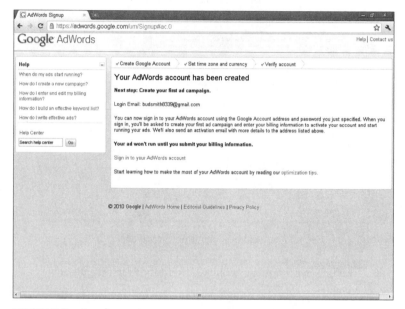

FIGURE 2.7   Google confirms the creation of your AdWords account.

10. Click the **Sign In to Your AdWords Account** link.

You are taken to the sign-in page for AdWords.

11. Test your account access; enter your password and click the **Sign In** button. Don't check the Stay Signed In check box unless you are sure that your computer can't ever be accessed by others.

The initial page of AdWords appears, with an invitation to create your first campaign. Using AdWords, including entering billing details, is described in the next lesson.

12. If you're finished with your Google account for now, click the **Sign Out** link.

You will want to get in the habit of signing out of your Google account when you're not at your computer to protect your business's confidential information and to prevent others from, for instance, changing your AdWords settings—which could be very expensive indeed.

CAUTION: **Log Out of Google and AdWords**
Your Google account allows access to your email and potentially your calendar, proprietary business documents, and more. Your AdWords account allows access to settings that could cause you to quickly incur thousands of dollars in charges. Develop the habit of logging out of your Google account and, especially, AdWords whenever you're going to be away from your computer.

In the next lesson, I show you how to set up your AdWords account, including billing options.

Summary

In this lesson, you learned what a Google account offers, why you should create a Google account for your business, how to sign up for your Google account while also creating a Gmail account, and how to sign up for an AdWords account.

LESSON 3

Creating Your First AdWords Campaign

In this lesson, you learn how to create your first ad campaign and launch it. You create settings for your campaign's location and language, write your first ad, choose keywords, set a budget, and set up billing. When you've finished, your ad campaign will launch.

Getting Started Fast

Google wants you to get going with your first ad campaign quickly. It's in Google's interest for you to start using the service—and spending money—right away. In most cases, this is probably a good idea. If you aren't really ready to use the service full-bore yet, you can at least set up a test campaign, spending little money while learning your way around AdWords.

An AdWords ad campaign is simply one or more ads and keywords grouped together for management and reporting purposes. You can group a given AdWords advertising effort into one or more campaigns, depending on your own preferences.

PLAIN ENGLISH: **Google AdWords Ad Campaign**

A Google AdWords *campaign* is a separately manageable group of advertisements that has its own reporting and statistics. It's flexible enough that you can use it in several different ways—one ad per campaign, or dozens. See Lesson 14, "Updating Your Campaign," for details.

AdWords presents you with a screen like the one shown in Figure 3.1. In this lesson, I take you through the steps to set up your campaign, as Google recommends. Along the way, I touch on many aspects of using AdWords—choosing keywords, creating effective ads—that I discuss in more depth in later lessons.

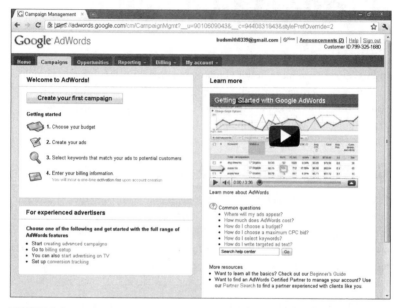

FIGURE 3.1   Google invites you to start right away on spending time—and money—on AdWords.

TIP: **Starting AdWords**

The quickest way to start AdWords is by going to http://adwords. com. Simply enter **adwords.com** in your browser's URL window.

Choosing Campaign Settings

Campaign settings are global settings for your entire campaign, which will include at least one ad and at least one keyword. The most important setting of all is your daily budget; try to decide what you can afford to experiment with before you get into the exercise of changing the settings.

Follow these steps to create your campaign settings:

1. If you're not there already, go to AdWords, and click the **Campaigns** tab to see the screen shown in Figure 3.1.

   The Campaigns tab appears with a Welcome to AdWords! heading.

   AdWords offers you answers to common questions, a Beginner's Guide, and more in the Learn More area.

2. If you like, take the time to learn more. Consider leaving the check boxes checked under Would You Like Extra Help? You will receive emails for ideas, special offers, and newsletters—you can always unsubscribe later if you choose.

3. Click the **Create Your First Campaign** button.

   A screen like the one shown in Figure 3.2 appears.

4. Set the campaign type.

   Campaign types are described in detail in Lesson 4, "Identifying Your Target Markets for AdWords." You can also learn about them by hovering your mouse over the question mark next to the Load Settings prompt, as shown in Figure 3.2.

   I recommend that you consider setting your first campaign for Search Network Only. This setting makes ads appear when users do a Google search, and is easiest to understand. It also runs up your bill more slowly than other, broader options.

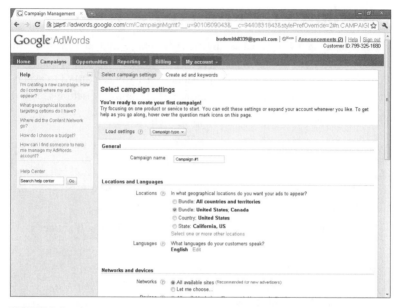

FIGURE 3.2   Create settings for your first campaign.

TIP: **Question Marks in AdWords**

Many of the choices you can make in AdWords are accompanied by a little question mark in a circle icon, as shown in Figure 3.2. Hover the mouse cursor over the question mark—then, in many cases, wait several seconds—and a tip will appear, often with a link to further information.

---

5. Enter a name for your campaign. Enter a name that will distinguish your campaign. If you later find yourself creating several similar campaigns, you can change the names as needed to show both similarities and differences.

6. Choose the ad location and language. Choose from among the locations given by clicking a radio button, or click the **Select One or More Other Locations** link to choose a particular location.

I recommend that you consider setting your first campaign for a small geographic area that you understand very well, such as the area immediately around your home or business. The area you choose should be one that's likely to be highly interested in your initial ad. This enables you to make sure that your advertising works for a well-known, prime audience before you spend very much money.

7. If you choose Select One or More Other Locations, an interactive map like the one shown in Figure 3.3 will appear. Use it to select the specific locations you want.

   Google suggests that you select areas at least 10 miles in diameter. See Lesson 6, "Deciding Where to Show Your Ads," for details on geo-targeting.

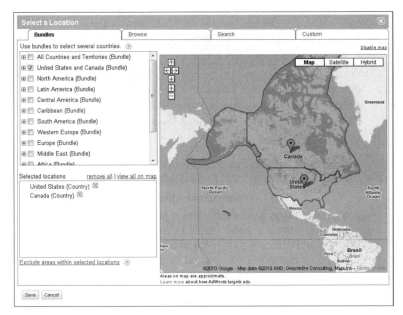

FIGURE 3.3   Google lets you select a location and more.

8. If you want to choose a language, click the **Edit** link next to Languages. Then choose a language.

The Languages choice means that your ad will display only for users who have chosen to use Google in a language that's the same one that you choose. In most areas, if you choose a language that isn't the default language for using Google in that area, you'll get very little traffic.

9. If you want to choose which networks to use, next to the Networks prompt, click the **Let Me Choose** radio button, as shown in Figure 3.4. Then choose whether to use Google search, search partners, or the Google display network.

   I recommend selecting only Google search for now because it's the easiest to understand and experiment with. See Lesson 4 for more about these options. Google recommends that you choose All Available sites, but I recommend beginning with Google Search as you'll spend less money while you're still on the steepest part of the learning curve.

10. If you want to choose which devices to use, next to the Devices prompt, click the **Let Me Choose** radio button. Then click the radio button to choose **Desktop and Laptop Computers**, for traditional computers, or **iPhones and Other Mobile Devices with Full Internet Browsers**, for smartphones. To fine-tune mobile options further, click the **Advanced Device and Carrier Options** link.

   I recommend choosing the default, **All Available Devices**, for your first campaign. If you want to manage your money carefully, choose the **Desktop and Laptop Computers** option, optimize your results there as described throughout this book; then create a separate campaign for mobile devices and optimize that separately.

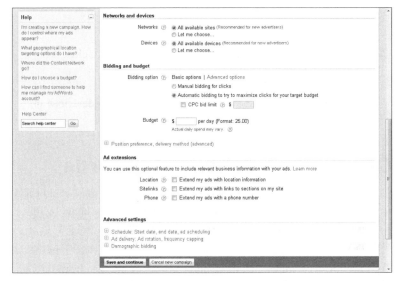

FIGURE 3.4   Your budget is the key consideration.

11. Choose your bidding option.

I recommend leaving the default choice in place, **Automatic Bidding to Try to Maximize Clicks for Your Target Budget**.

12. Enter your daily budget.

I recommend entering an amount that's significant enough to allow for some clicks, but not so significant as to seriously dent your pocketbook. You might try a fairly low amount such as $10 a day.

13. Consider entering other options: the position preference and delivery method (see Lesson 7); ad extensions such as location, site links, and phone number (see Lesson 8); and advanced settings for the schedule, ad delivery, and demographic bidding (see Lesson 9).

I recommend not changing these options for your initial campaign.

14. Review your choices. When you're happy with them, click the **Save and Continue** button.

The Create Ad and Keywords screen will appear, as described in the next section.

Creating an Ad and Keywords

Creating ads for AdWords and tying them to keywords is somewhat of a never-ending story; you can literally spend all your waking hours on this, and still never get it perfect. It's a lot of fun, though, after you get involved.

Try to follow basic rules, like those described here, and then learn through experimentation. As Thomas Edison once said, "Invention is 1% inspiration and 99% perspiration." The same is at least largely true for Google AdWords ad text and keyword choices.

Follow these steps to create initial ad text and keyword choices:

1. Follow the steps in the previous section to arrive at the Create Ad and Keywords screen, as shown in Figure 3.5.

2. Choose an ad type by clicking on a radio button next to **Text Ad**, **Image Ad**, **Display Ad Builder**, or **WAP Mobile Ad**.

I recommend you choose **Text Ad** for your initial ad. This type of ad is by far the most used on AdWords, and is the most important to gain experience with for most advertisers.

3. Next to the **Headline** prompt, enter a headline of 25 characters maximum.

The headline should be simple and descriptive. It should include one or more words that will show that the ad can meet the user's needs. For instance, *budget* will appeal to cost-conscious buyers; *five-star* will appeal to those seeking luxury.

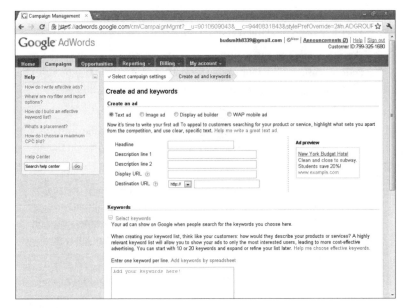

FIGURE 3.5   Create your first ad and choose one or more keywords to trigger it.

TIP: **Be Selective**

Don't worry about putting some people off with highly descriptive ad text. You pay for every click, so you want clicks only from the people who are most likely to follow through and buy from you.

---

4. Next to the **Description Line 1** prompt, enter the first line of your ad, using at most 35 characters.

There are many strategies for what to put in each line. I recommend that you consider using this simple strategy for the first line of your initial ad: List qualities of your product or service that remove objections. Such words and phrases as *clean*, *best value*, *highly rated*, and others assure customers that your product is worth consideration.

5. Next to the **Description Line 2** prompt, enter the second line of your ad, also 35 characters at most.

   For the second line of your ad, a simple strategy is a call to action: something about savings, timeliness, or both. *Mention this ad for 25% off* is one such approach; *only a few remaining* is another.

6. Next to the **Display URL** prompt, enter the URL of the website, or major area of a website, that users will visit, 35 characters maximum.

   The display URL is for helping users know where they're going; it should not, in most cases, be the exact URL they actually go to. So, enter your main website URL, such as www.sams.com, or, at most, the main site URL and one major subdirectory below that, such as www.sams.com/adwordsbook.

7. Next to the **Destination URL** prompt, enter the actual URL that users who click the ad will be directed to.

   The destination URL may be much longer and more elaborate than the display URL. However, the destination URL should be on the same site as the display URL; the destination URL should start with the display URL, and then add additional subdirectories, web page name, or database information as needed.

   The most effective campaigns have specific pages, called *landing pages*, to be used with one or more Google AdWords ads. You might not want to bother with this for now, in which case you should simply use a web page on your site that helps users get into a buying process.

8. Enter keywords, one per line, as shown in Figure 3.6. (See Lesson 11, "Finding Your Keywords," for more about keywords.)

   Enter keywords that you want your ad to display next to. For instance, for a wine shop, words such as *wine, wines, winery,* and the names of the top 10 or 20 best-selling wines in the shop are all potential keywords. So are the names of the shop, the owner, and even any clerks who are relatively well known. (You can count on employees to mention it if entering their name into Google brings up an AdWords ad for your business!)

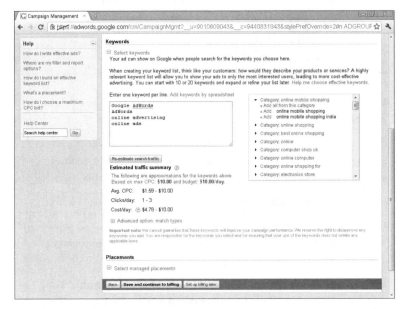

FIGURE 3.6 In AdWords advertising, keywords make the world go 'round.

Enter a keyword by itself for a broad match, including variations on a term. Enter the keyword in "quotes" for a specific phrase or a single word in [brackets] for a specific term. Enter a keyword with a minus sign in front of it to exclude that term. (For instance, if you want to advertise against searches for Bud Smith, the author, you might include "-baseball" to help exclude searches for Bud Smith, the baseball player.)

Google will suggest keywords for you. Be very careful in using them; they might just muddy the waters as to which keywords are generating traffic for you, without actually adding much.

9. Click the **Estimate Search Traffic** button.

TIP: **Use the Estimate Search Traffic Button Carefully**
Consider entering your list of keywords that you're considering in a separate document, such as a word processing document or spreadsheet. Then put the keywords into the AdWords Keywords area one at a time and click the **Estimate Search Traffic** button. This will give you estimates for each keyword separately, which you can use to decide which keywords to go with.

10. If you want, click the **Select Managed Placements** link to select placements in Google's content network.

I recommended earlier in this lesson that you eschew the content network for now, but if you want to use it, this option enables you to specify sites in the content network to use or not use.

11. Click the **Save and Continue to Billing** button to continue.

The Home screen will appear, with a request for you to enter your payment information. (If you are asked for your country or territory first, see the next set of steps.)

12. Click the **To Activate Your Account and Start Running Your Ads, Enter Your Billing Information** link to enter your billing information.

The Account Setup screen will appear, as described in the next section.

Setting Up Billing

Setting up billing for an online account is generally rather routine. However, you need to keep in mind three things with AdWords billing:

▶ Billing is open-ended. You can potentially spend hundreds or thousands of dollars on AdWords ads before you see much, if any, return from your AdWords efforts.

▶ Your AdWords ads stop running if your payment options run out of gas. This is not necessarily a bad thing.

▶ You should use business accounts, rather than personal accounts, to pay for any substantial AdWords activity, both to protect your personal finances and to keep your expenditures straight for tax purposes.

Follow these steps to set up AdWords billing:

1. Follow the steps in the previous section to arrive at the Account Setup screen.

2. Choose your country or territory from the pull-down menu. Click **Continue**.

   The screen for your billing contact information appears, as shown in Figure 3.7.

3. On the Set Up Your Billing Profile screen, enter information for your business (name, address, and so on). Click **Continue**.

   The screen for your payment options appears, as shown in Figure 3.8.

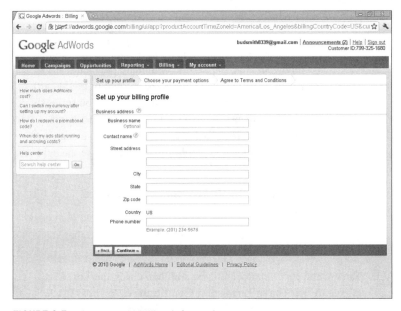

FIGURE 3.7   Enter basic billing information.

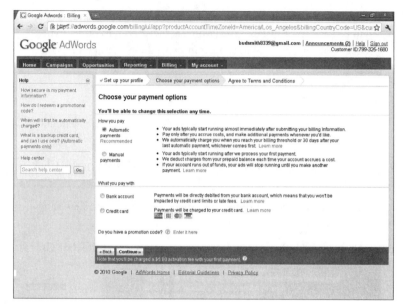

FIGURE 3.8   Enter payment options.

4. Choose a radio button: **Automatic Payments** or **Manual Payments**.

Google recommends that you choose automatic payments, in which money flows easily from your bank account or credit card to Google. It would, wouldn't it? I recommend that you seriously consider manual payments in the beginning of your AdWords efforts. You have to approve each transfer, giving you a chance to reconsider the effectiveness of AdWords for you before the next payment.

5. Choose a radio button: **Bank Account** or **Credit Card**. Then fill in the needed details. Click **Continue**.

You'll be shown terms and conditions (*T's and C's,* as they're called in the trade) for AdWords.

6. Review the terms and conditions, and then check the **Yes, I Agree to the Above Terms and Conditions** check box. Click the **Submit and Activate My Account** button.

Your account is created, and you're charged a one-time account activation fee of $5.00. You're then taken to the AdWords home screen, as shown in Figure 3.9.

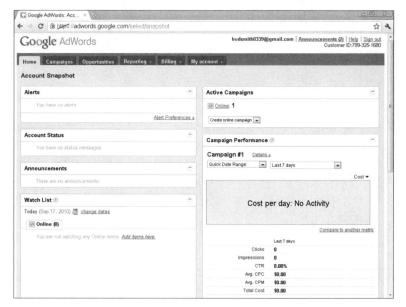

FIGURE 3.9   Your first campaign is running—but there's no information yet.

Your campaign has now launched! Statistics will come into AdWords a few hours after events occur.

CAUTION: **Billing Adds Up Quickly**

Part of the beauty of AdWords is that you can set it and forget it—but your bills add up every day. Check AdWords at least once a day to see your results. Work through the lessons in this book quickly so that you are getting the most out of AdWords.

Summary

In this lesson, you learned how to create your first ad campaign and launch it. You created settings for your campaign's location and language, wrote your first ad, chose keywords, set a budget, and set up billing. Your campaign has now launched.

LESSON 4

Identifying Your Target Markets for AdWords

In this lesson, you learn how AdWords is growing, and how to choose products and services to start selling via AdWords. You also learn how AdWords impacts customer decisions to buy from you and your type of business, and how to choose an initial campaign that's most likely to be profitable.

Starting with a Success

A Google AdWords ad campaign holds the promise of profitability for you. However, a campaign requires careful planning and measurement. You have to put in a fair amount of time up front, when you're learning, planning, and testing. The return for your efforts is likely to mostly occur in the future, as you get better at using AdWords and as AdWords and similar forms of advertising, especially on smart phones, continue to grow.

Figure 4.1 shows Google's quarterly revenues for 2006–2008. AdWords, which was launched in 2000, accounts for more than 90% of revenues in all the quarters. In the last quarter of 2008, revenues were $5.7B, and the year-over-year growth rate was 18%. This kind of large and steady growth rate for a multi-billion-dollar business is rarely seen; in fact, Microsoft, in its glory years, was probably the last such consistently large and fast-growing earner.

FIGURE 4.1   Google's AdWords business is growing fast.

What this means to you is that AdWords is an extremely successful business and that Google will do everything possible to keep growing it. Google's success is based on the success of its advertisers, so it is doing everything it can to make you successful.

This kind of success breeds imitators and other kinds of competitors, as well, but that's only a problem for Google, not for you. You can ignore unsuccessful imitators and competitors. The successful ones will simply represent additional advertising channels for you to consider. And, if you're successfully using AdWords over time, you're likely to be able to take advantage of new channels, as well.

However, from the start, you want your AdWords-based effort to succeed as much as possible. I suggest you set the goal of making a profit from your AdWords sales as close to the beginning of the campaign as possible. All sorts of techniques can help you increase your revenues if you're willing to take a loss on each sale. You need to prove to yourself that AdWords can actually help you make a profit, at least for some products or services and from some customers. Then you'll be motivated to expand your AdWords efforts where it makes cents (pun intended)—and dollars, as well.

How Do You Make Money?

So, now we've seen how Google makes money—and how much money it makes. How about you? How do you make money? Or, to put a fine point on it: What are the most profitable things you sell?

To get your AdWords advertising effort off to a good start, you want to identify products that are highly profitable and search friendly. (I describe more about what that means throughout this lesson.)

> PLAIN ENGLISH: **Gross Margin**
>
> A product's *gross margin* is the percentage of profit after subtracting only the buying-in cost, ignoring such factors as storage, returns, breakage, shrinkage, extra sales effort required, and so on. It's a rough but quick and useful measure of a product's profitability, and potentially of its importance to your business.

You might or might not know what your most profitable products are. In fact, you can identify highly profitable products in several complementary ways. For example, you want to consider products that

- ▶ **Have a high gross margin**. Take the amount of money you make per sale, after subtracting the buy-in cost of the product. If you sell a fancy chocolate bar for $5, and it costs you $2 to buy it in, the gross margin is 60%.

- ▶ **Have a high total profit**. Let's suppose you make only $1 on a less-fancy chocolate bar, but you sell 1,000 of them a month. That might be your most profitable single product as measured by gross profit.

- ▶ **Are easy to sell**. Sales effort eats into profits. Products that sell themselves, or that do a lot to attract customers to you, might, in a careful analysis, be more profitable than some products that have better gross margins or total profit.

▶ **Are growing quickly in sales.** If a product is growing quickly in sales, there's a land grab going on for sales of that product, and you need to grab your share of the available land. Such a product might contribute more to your profits in the longer term than your current steady sellers.

▶ **Are new, scarce, or seasonal.** There's usually some sense of buzz and excitement about new products, so they're great for AdWords advertising. Consider what's new among your offerings and whether now is the time to bring in something that you've been considering. Hard-to-find and seasonal products can have a new feel about them, too.

▶ **Can support a discounted or free offer.** The hottest words in marketing have long been said to be *new* and *free*. Do you have a product or service that lends itself to a free giveaway, or an offer with *free* in the name, such as a free trial, two for the price of one, and so on? If not free, can you discount a product heavily based on a manufacturer's promotion or similar consideration?

You don't have to do a strict analysis of the numbers involved before choosing one or more products for use with Google AdWords. You no doubt have a good, seat-of-your-pants feel for which products are hot without crunching the numbers.

TIP: **Fine-tune Your Campaigns**

The structure of Google AdWords is such that it's a real advantage to know everything possible about your costs and profitability per product, service, and so on. You can then use this information to fine-tune your AdWords campaigns. Don't let "paralysis by analysis" prevent you from getting started, but be ready to use AdWords and other tools to make your business more and more numbers-driven over time.

If you sell services, the analysis might be more difficult, depending on what you offer. Dog walking might be easy to analyze; dog bathing in your special doggie wash shop might be harder. And in any business, apportioning costs against different products or services can be maddening. However, you still need to identify what's hot.

Table 4.1 shows one possible chart for recording hot products/services. Note that the rankings are on a scale of one to five stars, with three stars being average. Using stars rather than strict dollar measures gives you a feel for hotness, rather than a detailed financial analysis.

TABLE 4.1 A Sample Chart for Hot Products/Services in a Candy Shop

Product	Chocolate Kisses	Regular Chocolate Bars	Fancy Chocolate Bars	Chocolate Bunnies
Gross margin	****	**	****	****
Total profit	*	****	****	****
Easy to sell	****	***	***	***
Fast growing	***	*	***	***
New/scarce/ seasonal	**	*	****	*****
Giveaway/discount potential	****	***	****	****
Consider?	No	No	Yes	Yes

Having a chart like the one in Table 4.1 enables you to identify the factors that are helping drive you toward advertising one product or service over another. It gives you a rational basis for making an initial decision and a point of comparison for evaluating your advertising against your results as they materialize.

You can create a similar chart for your own business and its products/services. Again, you can do detailed financial analysis or just use your own gut feel for what's hot and what's not.

NOTE: **Consider Google Places**

If you want to try a free Google advertising service before putting a lot of time and money into AdWords, consider setting up or improving your Google Places page, as shown in Figure 4.2. Your Google Places page can also complement your AdWords campaigns. See *Sams Teach Yourself Google Places in 10 Minutes* (Bud E. Smith, 2010) for details.

FIGURE 4.2   Google Places is another way for customers to find you.

How Do Customers Buy from You?

A profitability analysis can tell you what to consider selling using
AdWords. A look at how customers buy from you can tell you who might
be best reached by AdWords.

Here are the major ways that people might buy from you—and some
thoughts as to whether those selling approaches are AdWords friendly:

> ▶ **Online sales**. Online sales are by far the most AdWords-friendly
> type of sale. It's easy for the customer who sees your AdWords
> ad to complete the purchasing process quickly and conveniently,
> and it's easy for you to measure the entire process.

▶ **Phone sales or setting appointments by phone.** A greatly underrated technique for completing sales that start online, phone sales are quick, convenient, and feel secure to customers as compared to online buying. Setting appointments by phone is also an effective technique for (nearly) closing the sale. Phone sales also have a personal touch that online buying lacks.

TIP: **Use Phone Sales for Reorders**

Phone sales are particularly good for existing customers and particularly for reorders—neither of which, unfortunately, is a great fit with AdWords, which is more likely to reach new customers. Do use phone sales with existing customers, though, even if most of your customers come to your place of business (or you go to theirs).

▶ **Sales at the customer's location.** If you're willing to go visit your customer, and you can use AdWords to get the customer to set an appointment (online or by phone), your chances of making the sale might be quite high.

▶ **Sales at your location.** It's a lot easier for AdWords to drive an online sale or a phone call than to get customers to physically show up, except for mobile ads (which have to battle for just one or a couple of easily visible AdWords spots). Consider using a steep-discount coupon, a free offer, or other strong motivational tool. You should consider tracking the sale all the way through to completion to be part of the job, as well.

It's important to make it easy for customers to close the deal. The HumanWare website, which you can visit at www.humanware.com, for example, prominently displays the company's phone number on every page. Consider doing the same on your website.

To sum up, online sales are very AdWords-friendly, both making and tracking the sale. Making sales, or sales appointments, by phone is fairly AdWords-friendly, but you'll have to use some other means to track your sales success.

When the person who sees your AdWords ad has to come visit you to complete the sale, that's AdWords-unfriendly, as the person has to get up to do it. They may well put it off until the next time they're near you, and then forget. It's also hard for you to track, because you can't be sure how much influence the AdWords ad had on their decision to come in.

Identifying Your Type of Business

The way you use AdWords will vary depending on many factors, but the type of business you're in has a big effect. Here are some things to look out for, depending on your type of business:

- ▶ **Local store, generic products**. A local liquor store or grocery store needs people to know it's there. Getting a good search position on organic search is unlikely; local search might work better, and using Google Places is important. AdWords should be used sparingly, and only in the local area, to supplement organic and local search.

- ▶ **Local store, specialty products**. If you have a local store with specialty products, especially products with specialized keywords such as "left-handed screwdriver" or specific brand names, you need to get all the sales you can in your local area. Use AdWords strongly to complement organic and local search.

- ▶ **Shippable, generic products**. There's intense competition for broadly available products sold online, and it's come down to a price war. AdWords adds another dimension to the competition, often favoring big players. Employ AdWords judiciously so that your campaign doesn't become a financial drain.

- ▶ **Shippable, specialty products**. If you can be first in a niche, you can build up some degree of ownership of specialized products and the keywords that go with them. There's a good chance of success here, but you must carefully monitor profitability.

- ▶ **Local consulting, training, or other in-person services**. As with a specialty store, you need to get all the sales you can out of your local area. Strongly consider using AdWords, and think hard about potential keywords and ad copy to pull people in.

▶ **Consulting, training, and so forth over a broad area.** You might be willing to travel to do your consulting or training, but AdWords will make sense only if you have strong differentiation from providers based near to your customer. A San Francisco-based company, for instance, might be able to pull customers throughout Northern California; a San Diego-based one might have a hard time getting customers based in Los Angeles.

Choosing an Initial Campaign

The whole nature of online advertising, and AdWords features in particular, encourages you to do your online advertising the way an Internet expert with online selling capability would do it. That is, by choosing keywords that fit their business, by tracking from the AdWords ad click to the online sale, and then modifying the entire sales pipeline—the AdWords ad, the landing page, the ecommerce pages, even the products available for sale—to gradually improve AdWords performance.

The way that AdWords works encourages you to do online advertising for your business as if you were an Internet expert, doing your selling online. The technique is: choose keywords that fit your business; track from the AdWords ad click to the sale; then, continually modify the entire sales pipeline—the AdWords ad, the landing page, the ecommerce pages, even the products available for sale—to gradually improve AdWords performance.

> NOTE: **Locals Only?**
>
> If you run a local business, where most sales involve someone visiting your shop—or you visiting them—you might wonder if it's worth spending the time to develop AdWords ads when you're only reaching a small customer base. The answer is that more and more business is getting done through online and mobile connections with customers. Even as a local player, you need to get in the game. Proceed carefully, making at least a little bit of profit as you go, so as to hone your skills and build up this channel over time.

However, if you have a real-world business and are using AdWords to improve your sales, you are likely to be constrained by your physical location, by the line of business you're well established in, and by online and offline competition that might seem more attractive customers who are most likely to see your AdWords ad.

Many businesses depend on a slow sales process that involves multiple pre-purchase encounters with customers. If so, because you incur a cost for every click that users make on your AdWords ad, you want the AdWords click to have a high chance of actually closing a deal, which might mean targeting customers who have previously been exposed to your business in some way.

Check out online competition carefully. The easy availability and low prices of products available online can be quite discouraging, but don't despair. People still prefer to see or otherwise check out a product in person—and to buy from someone they physically interact with.

So, you need to consider whether you want to sell products to customers who are remote from you and need products shipped to them. For a bookstore, just about all the products can be shipped (although the competition is intense). For a chocolate shop, it's a mixed bag. For butchers, only specialized products—or high-margin products that support specialized shipping—work.

Luckily, AdWords supports *geo-targeting*: having your AdWords ads show up only to customers in certain specified locations. This is a great feature that helps you make a profit on your AdWords efforts early on.

A company called Business and Technical Communication Services (BATCS) is an example of the creative use of AdWords and geo-targeting. BATCS sells English pronunciation lessons and a book, *Get Rid of Your Accent*. They run AdWords ads only in certain parts of London. Figure 4.3 shows the Web page that appears when users click on the ad.

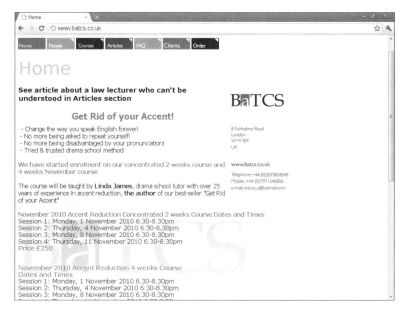

FIGURE 4.3   BATCS runs accent reduction classes in London.

The part of London where BATCS runs its ads is near where the company holds its classes and encompasses a dense array of English-language schools. This way, BATCS AdWords ads reach both potential book buyers and potential customers for pronunciation classes. When the AdWords budget is reduced, both book sales and calls inquiring about the classes drop. See Lesson 6, "Deciding Where to Show Your Ads," for details on geo-targeting.

BATCS could, of course, run ads throughout the United Kingdom; and if they were to do so, they would see some increase in book sales. However, distribution of the book is not as strong outside London, so many people might click the ad but not be able to easily buy. Also, the in-person courses would most likely be too far away for people outside of London. So, although running ads more broadly would bring in some revenue, doing so would not generate enough to pay for the ads. Only a narrowly focused ad campaign works for BATCS.

Consider these same factors as you develop your own AdWords campaign, especially when you're just starting out. Strategically target your ads, try to use "can't miss" keywords and geo-targeting, and keep your initial spending down. The goal is to gradually build up AdWords as a winning approach for you, one that you can grow with over time.

Summary

In this lesson, you learned that businesses are increasingly relying on AdWords and how to choose products/services to start selling via AdWords. You learned how AdWords impacts customer decisions to buy from you and your type of business, and how to choose an initial campaign that's most likely to be profitable.

LESSON 5

Setting Up a New Campaign

In this lesson, you learn how to set your campaign type, how to choose networks and devices for your ad to display on, and how to set the high-level options you need for your campaign, step by step.

Starting with Your Campaign Type

In Lesson 3, "Creating Your First AdWords Campaign," we created a campaign the "quick and dirty" way—making the choices that were most likely to be effective for a simple, possibly short-term campaign. Now it's time to set up a campaign more carefully, better explaining the choices available to you along the way.

When you first create a campaign, you have two choices, as shown in Figure 5.1:

▶ **Keyword-targeted campaign.** A keyword targeted campaign is tied to certain keywords that users enter. Your ad appears higher up on the page if you get a high number of clicks on your ad. This is by far the better known and more widely used type of AdWords campaign.

▶ **Placement-targeted campaign.** A placement targeted campaign is tied to the location on the page of your ad. Your ad appears higher up on the page if the landing page—the page that the user goes to when they click your ad—gets lots of visits. This can be caused by successful AdWords ads, but a popular page—such as the home page of an established business—can get lots of visits through word of mouth, organic search, and other means.

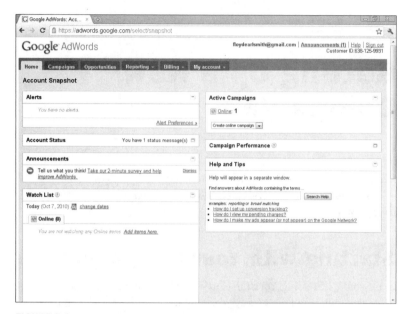

FIGURE 5.1   Choose a keyword-targeted approach for most campaigns.

NOTE: **Campaign Type and Networks and Devices**

All that choosing a campaign type does is to cause some of the options in the Networks and Devices part of the current page, Select Campaign settings, to be reset. However, you can change these settings to different values later, using the options described later.

TIP: **Placement-targeted Campaigns**

This book concentrates on keyword-targeted campaigns. A placement-targeted campaign is a less-used and, in some ways, more sophisticated type of ad. (You can more easily spend a lot of money for little return with placement-targeted campaigns.) Everything you learn in creating and running keyword-targeted campaigns will serve as useful preparation if you then decide to run placement-targeted campaigns.

After you choose a keyword-targeted or placement-targeted campaign, you're presented with a screen to select your campaign settings, as shown in Figure 5.2. You're asked for the campaign type. (Keyword-targeted versus placement-targeted is also a type of campaign, but AdWords doesn't call it that.)

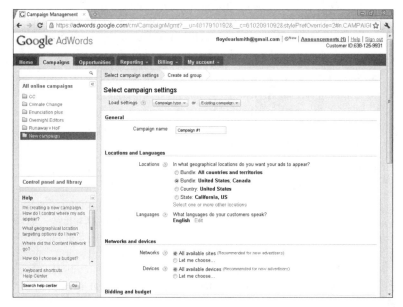

FIGURE 5.2   Search Network Only is the easiest campaign type to manage.

TIP: **Start with the Search Network Only**

Google AdWords gives you a lot of choices—but competition is heavy, so it's hard to get good results at first. One solution is to keep raising your budget. But instead of firing a shotgun—that is, using the Default option, which shoots a lot of pellets (dollars), but which might not get the penetration you need—consider a "rifle" strategy. This means starting with the Search Network Only option, getting good at that, and then adding other types of campaigns, always working to make your campaigns profitable.

AdWords offers a wide range of campaign types—but only some of them are useful:

▶ **Default**. This is the "leave it to Google" option. Google places your ads on both the Search Network and the Display Network (see the next two bullets for details). They appear on computers and mobile devices, as well. The reports you get break down your results for each. However, you give up control with this option; it might be better to create a Search Network campaign first, the simplest type, and then add other types as you gain confidence.

▶ **Search Network Only**. This is the original, simplest, and most common type of AdWords ad. Search Network ads show up alongside search results, as shown in Lesson 1, "Getting More Business with AdWords." You're in the scrum, battling for keywords, along with everyone else.

▶ **Display Network Only (Text Ads)**. This option places text ads in the Display Network—sites that allow Google to place AdWords ads in them, as shown in Figure 5.3. The program that site owners sign up for if they want to show Google Display Network ads is called AdSense. Most prestigious sites don't use AdSense, and most small sites don't bother—or aren't worth bothering with. So, you're left with your ad running in a broad middle class of sites that can be hard to get your head around.

PLAIN ENGLISH: **AdSense**

AdSense is the name of Google's program for site owners that enables them to place Google-powered ads on their sites and get paid when visitors click them. (If you choose to have your AdWords ads show up in Google's content network, AdSense controls how they display—I hope those Words make Sense!) AdSense is gradually growing more popular with site owners, who need to find ways to monetize—that is, to pay for, and to make money from—their sites.

FIGURE 5.3 Google's Display Network is a mix of big, medium, and small sites that display Google ads.

▶ **Display Network Only (Display Ad Builder).** You can use AdWords to build display ads, including graphics. These are relatively rare, but might be useful for some specific types of products or services. Consider experimenting with display ads after you've learned how to use text ads on the Display Network.

▶ **Mobile Devices Only.** Mobile devices are a fascinating field for advertising, but they show only the top one or two ads at a time on their small screens. So, if you get into this you have to, as Oakland Raiders owner Al Davis once said, "Just win, baby." Consider doing a separate mobile devices campaign as a trial after you gain expertise with Search Network ads.

▶ **Online Video (In-Stream) and Online Audio.** These multimedia choices demand an understanding of streaming media that's beyond most beginning online advertisers. For most businesses, I advise leaving these options to the experts until you become fairly accomplished with AdWords—or until your direct competitors start using them to take away "your" customers.

CAUTION: **Display Network**

I've found over time that my results for the Search Network were much better than for the Display Network, and that trying to improve my Display Network results was both a hassle and ultimately not very successful. You should probably try using the Display Network to test your results, but consider using a separate campaign just for the Display Network, and limiting the amount you spend until you can show that you're getting good results.

After you choose a campaign type, you need to give the campaign a name. This is actually hard to do because you might end up splitting your campaign into subcampaigns by type or keyword, and your keyword choices might change as you experiment, using Google's tools (see Lesson 6, "Deciding Where to Show Your Ads"). Consider choosing a name that reflects what you're trying to sell and the type of keywords you currently intend to use.

NOTE: **Choosing Locations and Languages**

AdWords offers Locations and Languages as the next set of options after you choose your campaign type and name your campaign. I recommend that you skip these choices and choose Networks and Devices, as described in the next section, because these choices are tied directly to the campaign type. Then go back to Locations and Languages, as described in the next lesson.

Choosing Networks and Devices

The Networks and Devices choices enable you to fine-tune—or even override—the choices you make when choosing the campaign type.

Google makes it easy to choose to advertise on all its networks, and all available devices. In a way, that's a good choice—there is a lot of opportunity to make money with AdWords on all of them, if you know what you're doing. However, you can also spend a lot during the learning curve.

So, I recommend that you take the time and trouble to study these options, and to make careful choices among them, learning one set of options at a time. Otherwise, your AdWords budget can disappear quite quickly. If you take the time to learn all the options up front, you can narrow your choices, and understand from the beginning just where your money is going.

> TIP: **Use Google Help**
>
> Google offers a great deal of help content as you work through AdWords. It might seem overwhelming at first, full of unfamiliar terms and ideas, but if you keep going back to it, it will gradually make more and more sense. Some of the best, most targeted context-sensitive help is available as pop-up windows, accessed by clicking the little question marks that show up on the AdWords screens, as shown in Figure 5.4. However, for some reason, it often takes forever for these tidbits to appear—I've waited anywhere from a couple of seconds to half a minute for them, which is ridiculous. However, it's usually worth the wait. I recommend that you keep clicking these little question marks as your knowledge grows.

The Networks option gives you crucial choices, some of which aren't visible unless you change the default setting. The default that Google gives you is All Available Sites. I recommend that, instead, you click **Let Me Choose.** You'll see the choices shown in Figure 5.4:

▶ **Search – Google Search.** This check box means your ad can appear on Google's search results page for keywords that you choose, if your other choices (such as location, time of day, budget, and so forth) allow it. This is the option people usually think of when they think of AdWords ads.

▶ **Search – Search Partners.** This option is available only if you enable Google search, as described in the previous bullet. It enables your ad to show up on partner sites that use Google search, a common enough choice. These are not necessarily sites that people go to with searching in mind, and they might be searching within that particular site. So, I recommend that you turn this option off initially, and then add it in as a test when you're getting good results from a Google search-only strategy.

▶ **Display – Display Network.** This is the same choice described in the previous section; it puts your ad on sites that use AdSense, and on YouTube, Gmail, and other Google properties.

▶ **Relevant Pages – Across the Entire Network**. This option shows your ads across all relevant properties on the Display Network. You get potentially broad coverage, but no control.

▶ **Relevant Pages Only on the Placements and Audiences I Manage**. This option gives you a lot of control, but can also potentially take a lot of time. If you're advertising in a very specific segment and have a good idea what sites you want, it's a good choice. If not, it might be too time-consuming to be worth the effort.

FIGURE 5.4   Carefully choose which networks and devices you advertise on.

The Devices option also gives you choices, including some very detailed ones, which are only available if you select Let me choose. These options are also shown in Figure 5.4:

▶ **Desktop and Laptop Computers**. These devices have larger screens and can show more ads, so you can use a sophisticated strategy for placing your ad. One such strategy might be paying less per click, and allowing your ad to sometimes appear in the fourth or fifth position among the AdWords ads—your ad will still be seen on the vital first page of results.

▶ **iPhones and Other Devices with full Internet Browsers**. This option includes the mobile phones generally known as *smart phones*—the iPhone, Android-powered phones such as Motorola's Droid family, BlackBerries (many of which have quite small screens), and others.

▶ **Advanced Device and Carrier Options**. This option lets you target only specific devices—even just the iPad! Usually the idea is that you would have different ad content or ad types for different devices, but if you have an iPad-specific product, that works too. You can also target specific mobile phone carriers; the list of choices you're presented is relevant to the geography you're working in, not where you target your ads to show (as described in the next lesson).

Setting the Campaign Type and Related Options

The information in the previous parts of this lesson is meant to help educate you in the possibilities of creating a campaign. This part takes you through the steps, one at a time. See the previous information for details.

The AdWords campaign is flexible, and can be used in many ways. You can create a single campaign for each individual ad; for more or less closely related, and larger or smaller, groups of ads and keywords; or for everything you ever do in AdWords.

I recommend a layered approach. Your techniques and goals for Google search and the Google Display Network are different enough that I recommend separate campaigns for those. I recommend additional, separate campaigns for computers versus smart phones (with the importance of being in the top or second position so much higher on the latter) and—by necessity—for display ads, in-stream online video and online audio.

It's mostly up to you, though; you can use campaigns for a very narrow or a very broad approach to AdWords.

With that thought in mind, follow these steps to create a campaign:

1. If you're not there already, go to AdWords, and click the **Home** tab to see the screen shown in Figure 5.1, earlier.

   The home page appears with the title Account Snapshot.

2. Under the Active Campaigns header, pull down the menu Create Online Campaign. Choose **Keyword Targeted** or **Placement Targeted.** Keyword Targeted is the right choice for most campaigns. The Campaigns tab opens, and the heading Select Campaign Settings appears.

3. From the Campaign Type pull-down menu, choose the campaign type: **Default, Search Network Only**, **Display Network Only (Text Ads)**, **Display Network Only (Display Ad Builder)**, **Mobile Devices Only**, **Online Video (In-Stream)**, or **Online Audio**.

   For several of the choices—Default, Search Network Only, Display Network Only (Text Ads), or Mobile Devices Only—the campaign type you choose causes specific options to be preset in the Networks and Devices area. The choices you then make in the Networks and Devices area can fine-tune, or even override, the specific choice you make from the Campaign Type pull-down. See steps 5–8.

4. Enter the campaign name, up to 30 characters. Skip Locations and Languages for now; it's covered in Lesson 6.

> NOTE: **The Name Game**
> Naming is difficult at this point, because you might make decisions that change the nature of the campaign along the way. However, you can change the name at any point in the future, without causing problems, just by clicking the campaign name in the Campaigns tab.

5. Under Networks and devices, next to the Networks prompt, click the radio button for **Let Me Choose.** A range of choices appear, with the options preset by your choice of campaign type, as described in step 3.

6. Under the Networks option, for Search, use the check box to specify whether to display ads in the **Google Search** network. If you set this check box, you also can then use a check box to additionally display ads in the **Search Partners** network, or you can leave this choice clear.

NOTE: **Google Search Network Required**
You must enable ads in the Google Search network to have the option to also display them in the Search Partners network.

---

7. Under the Networks option, for Display, use the check box to specify whether to display ads in the **Display Network.** If you set this check box, you can then the radio buttons to use **Relevant Pages Across the Entire Network** or use **Relevant Pages Only on the Placements and Audiences I Manage.**

TIP: **What They Really Mean**
The first radio button choice (Relevant Pages Across the Entire Network) basically means "let Google handle it." The second choice (Relevant Pages Only on the Placements and Audiences I Manage) is more likely to lead to good results, but can be a lot of work.

---

8. For Devices, click the radio button for **Let Me Choose.**

   A range of choices appear, with the options preset by your choice of campaign type, as described in step 3.

9. Under the Devices option, use the check boxes to include **Desktop and Laptop Computers** and/or **iPhones and Other Mobile Devices with Full Internet Browsers.**

TIP: **Separate Is Better**
I recommend that you take advantage of these options to create separate campaigns for the first choice, Desktop and Laptop Computers, as opposed to the second choice, iPhones and Other Mobile Devices with Full Internet Browsers. That's because the importance of being in the first one or two positions is so much greater on smart phones, with their small screens. My suggestion

is that you first optimize the cost-effectiveness of your campaign for computers and then, using the knowledge you gain, create a separate, winning (that means "profitable") campaign on smart phones.

10. If you enabled iPhones and Other Mobile Devices with Full Internet Browsers, click the link **Advanced Device and Carrier Options.** The available options for an advertiser based in North America are shown in Figure 5.4. (The options don't change even if you geo-target your campaign for some other continent, as described in the next lesson.) I recommend that you inspect the available options, shown in Figure 5.4, but not change them unless you have a very good reason to do so. (Hatred of one of the carriers, based on your own experience of dropped calls, overfilling, and so on, is usually not sufficient reason to cut them out of your advertising plans.)

11. Continue with setting the other options on this page, as described in Lesson 6, "Deciding Where to Show Your Ads," (for geo-targeting), Lesson 7, "Setting Your Bidding, Budget, and Delivery Options," (for your budget), and Lesson 8, "Adding Extensions," (for extensions and advanced settings). For now, enter a minimal amount for the budget—perhaps $1 a day—and click the button, Save and Continue. Then proceed to Lesson 6.

You can stop and take a break now, but be sure to return soon to complete the ad; you'll be paying a small amount per day for an ad without all its options fully set until you do.

Summary

In this lesson, you learned how to set your campaign type, how to choose networks and devices for your ad to display on, and how to set the high-level options you need for your campaign, step by step.

LESSON 6

Deciding Where to Show Your Ads

In this lesson, you learn why it's a good idea for many new AdWords advertisers to target their advertising to a limited area at first to cut costs and maximize conversion ratios. You also learn the many clever ways that AdWords offers you for interactively setting your geographic targets and how to target a campaign for various language settings.

Understanding Why Geo-Targeting Works

Geo-targeting is a fairly new capability for the Web. It used to be that website creators and advertisers had no way to know where a specific user was when she connected. There were ways to guess, but they were imprecise, and services such as AOL aggregated users into one giant blob that seemed to all be located wherever AOL's servers were.

No longer. Google uses a number of means to guesstimate where a user is coming from, and then shows the user this guesstimated location in services such as Google Maps. If Google has it wrong and the user doesn't correct Google's misimpression, the user keeps getting useless local search results until he fixes it.

So, Google's understanding of where users are is already good and steadily getting better. But, given that Google knows where (most) users are, why do you want to geo-target information? Doesn't cutting some people out mean losing customers?

Yes, but the point of geo-targeting is that every click a user makes on your ad costs you money. So, you want to eliminate clicks from unlikely buyers and preserve clicks from likely buyers. That way, you cut out a lot of cost while keeping most of your revenue. The result: turning a healthy profit.

Here's an example. Let's say I sell business consulting services to "green" businesses in Oakland, California. There's no hard limit on who might buy from me—but the fact is, the closer someone is to me, the more likely that the person will buy my services. I share more local information and perspective with them, it's easier and cheaper for us to meet, and they are more likely to know one of my past or current clients. All these factors give me a local advantage.

With that in mind, let's do the (imaginary) math for a consulting ad. See Table 6.1 for specifics.

TABLE 6.1   Assumed Profitability of AdWords Ads for Oakland-Based Consulting

	Oakland	SF Bay Area (– Oakland)	California (– SF Bay Area)	All of U.S. (– Calif.)
Population	400,000	6.6M	30M	280M
Clicks (at .1% of population)	400	6,600	30,000	280,000
Cost per click	$1	$1	$1	$1
Total cost	$400	$6,600	$30,000	$280,000
Conversion ratio (from click to buy)	10%	1%	0.1%	0.01%
Total customers	40	66	30	28
Profit per customer	$1,000	$1,000	$1,000	$1,000
Total profit	$40,000	$66,000	$30,000	$28,000
Total cost	$400	$6,600	$30,000	$280,000
Gross profit	$39,600	$59,400	0	–$252,000
Sum of profits	$39,600	$99,000	$99,000	–$153,000

PLAIN ENGLISH: **Conversion Ratio**

A *conversion ratio* is the number of people who take some desirable step in the transition from potential customers to actual customers. It can describe a multistep process, as with seeing your ad online all the way through to making a purchase, or a single step, such as from seeing your ad to clicking it. Improving your conversion ratio at each step in the purchase process is the key to improving your profitability with AdWords.

It can be hard to read tables of data if you're not used to it, so let me put this into words. Here's what happens as I advertise more and more broadly:

▶ **Oakland only.** One-tenth of 1% of the population clicks my ad. That's 400 people, at $1 per click, so my cost is $400. Because I'm local, 10% of people who click buy from me, or 40 customers. I make $1,000 per client, or $40,000, and only spend $400. My profit is nearly $40,000. Wow! But I want more income, so I advertise in the whole San Francisco Bay Area.

▶ **SF Bay Area only.** The additional 6.6 million people outside Oakland still click at the same rate, costing me $6,600. (Remember, that bill has to get paid way before I get paid by my clients.) Because I'm not truly local, only 1% buy from me. This still brings in $66,000, so my profit is nearly $60,000—on top of my nearly $40,000 from Oakland. Wow! I'm a six-figure consultant!

▶ **The rest of California.** Expanding to all of California, I get 30 million more target customers, and their clicks cost me $30,000. I'm not local at all, so only 0.1% buy from me. This brings me 30 customers, making me $30,000—so I break even in California outside the Bay Area. (Actually, I lose in terms of cash flow because I have to pay AdWords up front, but only get paid after the fact by my clients.)

▶ **The rest of the United States.** The good news is that I get 280 million more target customers. But their clicks cost me $280,000! The rest of America thinks Californians are wackos, and I'm far away, so only 0.01% buy from me. This only brings me 28 customers—about the same as non-Bay Area California did—but I lose about a quarter of a million dollars on this expanded audience.

CAUTION: **Biting Off Too Much**

The way that AdWords works makes it easy to choose a wastefully large target area for your ads, and then generate big bills while you puzzle over results that are mildly encouraging, in that you do get some business, yet are loss-inducing overall. Use geo-targeting, as described in this lesson, to target a small area initially, and then build your targets up over time.

If I look at this for my whole business, I would make about $40,000 a year from Oakland only. My profit grows to about $100,000 a year from Oakland plus the rest of the San Francisco Bay Area. And it stays exactly the same for all of California. But I lose about $150,000 a year if I advertise across the United States.

This is, of course, a made-up and simplified example. If I put the word "Oakland" in my ad—or the much longer phrase "SF Bay Area"—I'll cut down on clicks from people far away. But I'll have used up my ad space, and the clicks probably won't drop off enough to avoid some cost.

The only way to really know if you're getting the most out of AdWords, though, is to experiment. Try different advertising copy, in different places, with different offers. Mix and match and find what works.

However, when you're starting out, you're really only trying to answer one burning question: Can AdWords make money for me?

What you're looking for when you start is what's called an *existence proof*—real evidence of AdWords bringing in new business for you, profitably. So, when you're getting started, don't pick a big target marketing area for your AdWords ads and then think about cutting it back. Pick a small area, where you're local to your customers, and get started there. Make that small area profitable through your ads, your landing page, and your conversion to a sale. Then expand your AdWords reach to larger areas.

Think of each small area that you put your AdWords ads in as putting up a billboard in that area. You wouldn't pay for 1,000 billboards with new, untested art and message on them. Instead, you'd put one billboard out, try it, see what people thought. Then you'd experiment, get the "creative" right, and only then roll out the billboard campaign broadly (and pay the resulting bills).

> TIP: **Begin with Narrowcasting**
>
> Don't start your AdWords campaign with a big target area. Pick a small area where you have an advantage of some sort—you're well known, you're local, lots and lots of your target customers live there, or similar qualifiers. Test your AdWords skills and selling effectiveness in the small area, where the odds are stacked in your favor, and then only roll it out more broadly when you know you're making a profit.

Using AdWords for Geo-Targeting

AdWords lets you geo-target down to a fine level of detail, although the exact "resolution" varies by location. You can certainly target down to the level of a medium-sized city such as Oakland (population 400,000) with no trouble, and even grab chunks of the adjacent cities Berkeley and Alameda, for instance, if you'd like.

AdWords also lets you combine quite different target areas in a single campaign. For instance, you can get a list of high-income neighborhoods, which are spread out very unevenly, and choose to target all of them in one campaign.

However, if you want to have different strategies for different parts of your overall target areas group—for instance, different ad text and different keyword bidding amounts for areas close to you versus those that are far away—you need different campaigns.

> TIP: **Local Targeting for Expansive Campaigns**
>
> Even if your sales campaign and your presence are intended to be national or global, starting out in a restricted geographic area helps you get up to speed before committing big bucks. And you still can consider using your local area as a test market—you're likely to know its idiosyncrasies well, allowing you to get the most bang for your buck.

You use a dialog called Select a Location to build up your list of targeted areas. It has four tabs, each of which works differently:

▶ **Bundles.** This is the big picture—continents and countries. After you choose a continent or a country, though, you can exclude countries, states or provinces, metro areas (that is, multicity agglomerations such as Los Angeles), or specific cities.

▶ **Browse.** The Browse tab gives you a list of countries, and then enables you to choose or exclude states or provinces, metros, and cities.

▶ **Search.** The Search tab enables you to search for a specific area, including countries, states or provinces, metro areas, and even ZIP codes. It has limits, though; when I searched for Rockridge, a neighborhood in Oakland, it didn't return a result. When I searched for Rockridge, CA, it returned Oakland.

▶ **Custom.** The Custom tab enables you to really fine-tune where your ads display, and I recommend it for use when you're getting started. By using the Custom tab, you can get the most precise control over where your ads show up. In some countries, including the United States, Canada, the United Kingdom, and Germany, you can allow the address of your business to show underneath ads that are geo-targeted using the Custom option. This is a confidence builder for local businesses, and I recommend that you use it as such if it's available to you.

You can use all these tabs together to build up the list of targeted areas for your ad. Follow these steps to geo-target a campaign with AdWords:

1. If you're not there already, go to AdWords and start creating a new campaign, as described in the previous lesson. Choose the campaign type, give your campaign a name, and set the advertising networks and devices to run your ads on.

You should be on the Campaigns tab, with the Select Campaign Settings area displayed, as shown in Figure 5.2 in the previous lesson.

2. Under the Locations and Languages area, next to the prompt, Locations, click the link **Select One or More Other Locations.**

The Select a Location dialog opens, as shown in Figure 6.1. An area will already be selected.

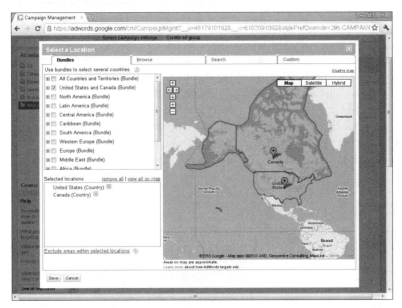

FIGURE 6.1   The Select a Location dialog lets you target all sorts of locations, large or small.

3. Use the Bundles tab to add the whole world, or a continent-sized area (called a *bundle* by AdWords). Click the check box next to a continent's (bundle's) name. To add a specific country, click the + sign next to the bundle name, and choose specific countries from the list that appears. The names of the countries you select appear in the Selected Locations area.

4. To remove a country from the targeted group, click the **red X** next to its name in the Selected Locations area. Alternatively, click a country that's highlighted in blue on the map, and then click the **Don't Show Ads Here** prompt that appears. The country will be removed from the Selected Locations area.

TIP: **Building a List of Excluded Countries**
You can create a list of specific countries to exclude by choosing one or more bundles, and then pruning unwanted countries, or by building up the list one country at a time.

5. Use the Browse tab, shown in Figure 6.2, to add countries, states or provinces, metro areas, and cities. Click the plus sign next to a country's name to add it. To add a specific state or province, metro area, or city, click the check box next to a country's name, find the area you're looking for, and then click the check box to add it. Alternatively, for areas that have been individually selected, click an area that's highlighted in blue on the map, and then click the **Don't Show Ads Here** prompt that appears. The Selected Locations area displays the results of your work, potentially combining continents and much smaller areas.

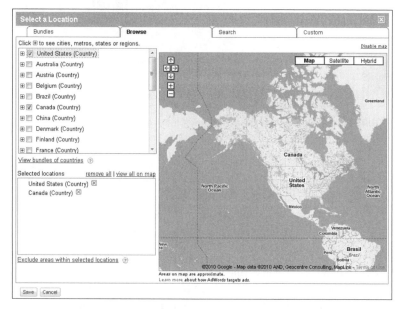

FIGURE 6.2 The Browse tab allows access to countries, states and provinces, metro areas, and cities.

PLAIN ENGLISH: Don't Add Everything Then Expect to Trim

You can't exclude a smaller area that's part of a larger area you've selected. (For example, you can't choose the entire United States and then poke holes in it like a slice of Swiss cheese.) To include or exclude small areas, you have to work by addition of each small area, not subtraction of small areas from a larger whole.

---

6. Use the Search tab, shown in Figure 6.3, to add specific areas of varying sizes. Enter the name of the area (down to the city level), and AdWords returns one or more areas that fit the name. Search works on bundles, countries, states and provinces, metro areas, and cities.

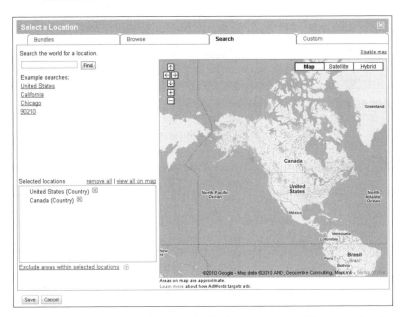

FIGURE 6.3   The Search tab gives you flexible access to different kinds of areas.

▶ If you enter the name of a continent, AdWords displays the continent with a tag for each country displayed on the map, like pushpins, as shown in Figure 6.4.

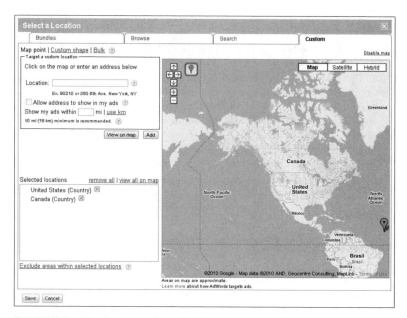

FIGURE 6.4   The Custom tab really lets you get specific.

> ▶ If you enter the name of a local area within a city, along
>   with the state or province, AdWords might return the city
>   or metro area of which that local area is a part.

7. Use the **Map Point** option of the Custom tab, shown in Figure
   6.4, to add specific areas around an address or ZIP code. Enter
   the address or ZIP code and a number for the radius within which
   to show ads. Choose **Miles** or **Kilometers.** If the location is an
   address (not a ZIP code), you can, if it's offered, click the check
   box **Allow Address to Show in My Ads** to turn this option on.
   (Recommended, if it's practical for you.)

TIP: **Precise Targeting Is Possible**

The Custom tab doesn't enable you to do precise ZIP code marketing; it treats a ZIP code as a specific point within the ZIP code
area, rather than as an area in its own right. It does, however,
enable you to set the radius around a ZIP code center point or
address to as little as 1 mile, so you can get quite precise in your
targeting.

8. Use the Custom Shape option of the Custom tab, shown in Figure 6.5, to draw selection areas. Click the **Custom Shape** link, and then click the polygon on the map. Click the map to set points. Or enter GPS coordinates, one pair per line, to specify the points. Click **View on Map** to see the area displayed. Click **Show Ads Here** to add the area to the Selected Locations list.

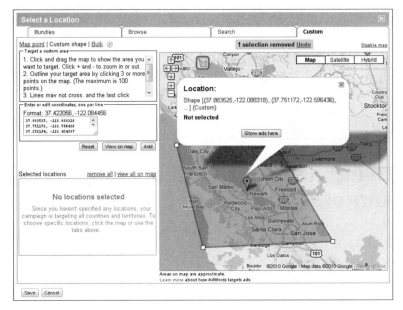

FIGURE 6.5   You can gerrymander your own AdWords targeting area.

AdWords creates a polygon (a pointy shape) connecting the points you enter by clicking or by entering GPS coordinates.

9. Use the Bulk option to enter up to 100 locations. Click the **Bulk** link, and then enter the names of locations—countries, cities, ZIP codes, and so forth—one per line. Click **View on Map** to see the area displayed. Click **Add** to add the area to the Selected Locations list.

ZIP codes are mapped to the nearest city.

10. Click the **View All on Map** link to see all the areas you've entered and review them. If needed, take a screenshot of the map to share with others. Change your selections if needed. If needed, press Alt+PrtSc, or similar key combination, to take a screenshot of the map; paste it into a Word document or email message to share and discuss with others. When you've finished, click **Save**.

Your choices are saved and displayed next to the Locations prompt on the Select Campaign Settings screen.

CAUTION: **Biting Off Too Little**

If you choose a small geographic target and an obscure keyword, such as "toy petrosaurs," you won't get many clicks. Stay on top of your AdWords ads in the early days to make sure you're not wasting your time with too precise a degree of fine-tuning.

Using AdWords for Language Targeting

AdWords enables you to target your campaign to customers who have set their Search Language setting on Google to a specific value in Google's Search Preferences area. Setting the Search Language to a specific language means that pages written in that language are ranked higher in Google's search results.

Unfortunately for you as a marketer, not every customer who speaks a given language will set his or her search preferences to that language. Anecdotal evidence indicates that not many Google users know about this option or bother with it. Customers might even know about the option, but prefer to see the same results as speakers of the default language for that area—they might then even translate the page into their preferred language.

Geography could take care of much of the problem for you. In that case, think carefully about whom you're trying to reach in a given area and what kind of ads you should present to them.

Given these considerations, it's probably best to experiment cautiously with the language option. Consider setting up a campaign in the majority language for a country or region, and then a campaign in the less-used language, with all the other settings (except for the language targeted) identical. Compare the results, and make sure that you're getting traction in the less-used language before investing a lot of effort.

Follow these steps to set the target language for your campaign in AdWords:

1. If you're not there already, go to AdWords and start creating a new campaign, as described in the previous lesson. Choose the campaign type, give your campaign a name, and set the advertising networks and devices to run your ads on.

   You should be on the Campaigns tab, with the Select Campaign Settings area displayed.

2. Under the Locations and Languages area, next to the prompt, Languages, click the **Edit** link.

   A list of languages appears. A language will already be selected.

3. Click to set the check box next to the languages that you want to target your ads against. Note that AdWords won't translate your ad text for you.

4. Continue to setting your budget, as described in the next lesson.

CAUTION: **Spelling in Foreign Languages**

Be careful when creating ad content or landing page content in languages other than your native tongue. Spelling errors, grammatical mistakes, even a seemingly odd tone can be quite irritating or confusing to potential customers, actually doing you and your company more harm than good. Get help from skilled native speakers to get your content right.

Summary

In this lesson, you learned why it's a good idea for many new AdWords advertisers to target their advertising to a limited area at first to cut costs and maximize conversion ratios. You also learned to use various techniques for interactively setting your geographic targets and how to target a campaign for various language settings.

LESSON 7

Setting Your Bidding, Budget, and Delivery Options

In this lesson, you learn how bids for search keywords work and how strong ad copy helps your ad get shown more. You then learn how to set options for bidding for keywords, specifying your ad budget, and delivering your ads.

Understanding Keyword Bids and Winning Ads

AdWords uses an interesting, economical, but somewhat difficult-to-understand process for deciding exactly whether your ad shows up next to the search results when the user enters a keyword you've bid on.

The key items are the keyword you use, the amount you bid to show your ad when a user enters that keyword, the amount you pay when your ad is clicked, and your budget. Here's an oversimplified description of how they interact:

1. You bid on a keyword—let's say it's "english pronunciation." (You need to focus your bids—by keyword or phrase, and, optionally, geographically—to keep your bids from being too high.)

    Figure 7.1 shows an example of a search for the term "english pronunciation," along with the many ads that appear along with the search results.

Maximum bid 80 cents; next lower
bid is 60 cents. Amount paid: 61 cents

Maximum bid $1; next lower bid is
80 cents. Amount paid: 81 cents

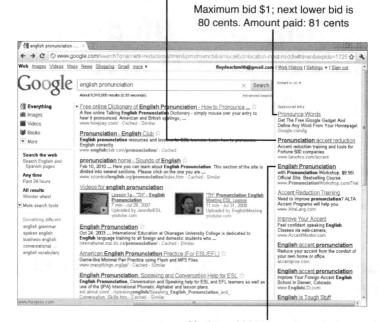

Maximum bid 60 cents; next lower
bid is 40 cents. Amount paid: 41 cents

FIGURE 7.1   Google uses maximum bids to choose winners, and then
charges less.

2. You bid an amount (or let AdWords manage the bidding for you).
Perhaps you bid $1 a click. If you have the highest bid on that
keyword, your ad wins, and is the top AdWords ad for that page.
AdWords places the ad in the top position on the right side of the
search results page or even, if you're lucky, above the search
results.

If your bid is the second highest, you get the second position;
third highest, third position; and so on.

3. AdWords checks your payments against your daily AdWords
budget. Perhaps it's $25. In this example, after 25 clicks in a day
(approximately), AdWords stops running your ad.

There's one confusing part that saves you money: the use of your bid amount as a maximum bid. If you bid $1, and someone else bids 80 cents, you win. But you don't pay $1 when users click your ad. Instead, you pay 81 cents—just enough to beat the next-lower bid. This saves you 19 cents per click.

Imagine that five people bid on the keyword "longboards," and they bid 20 cents, 40 cents, 60 cents, 80 cents, and $1. All five ads show, and the advertisers pay 1 cent, 21 cents, 41 cents, 61 cents, and 81 cents. Each advertiser pays just enough to beat the next-lower bid—and each advertiser saves 19 cents on each showing of their ad.

If there are bids just 1 cent apart—say, $1, 99 cents, 98 cents, and so on—every advertiser pays the amount they bid. The bid amount is the maximum they pay; the amount they actually pay is 1 cent more than the next-higher maximum bid.

Now that's a bit complicated—and it's also oversimplified. As AdWords shows various ads, it monitors how often they get clicked. AdWords doesn't just show the ad with the highest bid on a given keyword. It shows the ad with a high bid that gets clicked a lot.

You see, Google is not interested in getting the most money for one click. It's interested in getting the most money for all the clicks combined. So, an ad with a bid of 60 cents that gets clicked on 20 times in a day earns Google $12. It beats an ad with a bid of $1 that gets only 10 clicks, earning Google $10.

PLAIN ENGLISH: Quality Score

Your ad's *quality score* is the product of the amount that you pay for users' clicks (based on the maximum bidding approach) and the number of clicks it gets. A frequently clicked ad that pays less per click can beat less-enticing ads with higher maximum bids.

This system is confusing, but it works for the AdWords environment as a whole. You're motivated not only to get your bids right, but to create ads that entice people to click them (see Lesson 10, "Writing Great Ads"). Google makes lots of money, so it keeps improving its search engine, the AdWords system, and so on. In the big picture, everyone wins.

There is one notable fly in the ointment. After a group of ads is established, generating lots of money for Google and lots of clicks for the advertisers, it's hard for a new ad to break in. The recommended way to beat this potential trap is, first, to test your copy until it's as strong as humanly possible. The next step is then, sadly, to overbid at first, spending a chunk of money up front to get your ad established. Only when the ad has broken in to the group of successful ads can you manage your bidding downward to avoid paying more than you really have to for clicks (for instance, to settle for a middle position in the list of ads, at moderate cost, rather than gunning for the top position, with the highest cost, every time).

> TIP: **Planned Overbidding**
> You might have to overbid on a keyword at first to increase your Quality Score so that you can get your ad established among the successful ads. However, this requirement is true at this writing; Google might make adjustments to reduce or eliminate the need to do this. See Lesson 16, "Using Additional Reports and Tools," for details.

Using Basic Bidding Options

Bidding for your AdWords ad placements is tricky and potentially expensive. Your bids can help your ads get seen and clicked by the right people, or you can pay too much for clicks that don't bring in enough revenue. Your ad bids can even contribute to your ads hardly running at all.

You need to concentrate on three major parts of the online selling funnel as you consider your bids:

► **Cost per click**. This is the cost to you when a user clicks your ad. It's usually an amount less than the maximum bid that you enter, unless the bids are just 1 cent apart (see the previous section).

> NOTE: **Cost Per Placement**
> In addition to cost per click (CPC) advertising, where you pay each time the user clicks your ad, AdWords offers cost per placement advertising, in which you pay each time your ad is shown. (The abbreviation used, CPM, means "cost per thousand placements.")

CPC is far more popular, and is almost certainly your foundational strategy for using AdWords. CPM advertising is generally a supplemental strategy, best pursued with a smaller part of your ad budget, in a way that draws on what you learn from CPC and is complementary to it. I don't discuss CPM in detail in this book.

▶ **Profit per sale.** This is the amount of profit you make when an ad results in a sale. If you want to take a longer-term focus, you can calculate the net present value of a new customer, the percentage of your AdWords-derived customers who are new—which is probably quite high—and look at that instead of the profit from a single sale.

PLAIN ENGLISH: **Net Present Value**

The *net present value*, or NPV, of a new customer is the total profit that you'll ever earn from that customer, discounted (reduced) to account for the fact that much of the profit won't be realized for some time to come. (A bird, or a dollar, in the hand is worth two in the bush, as the saying goes.) For instance, if you expect to make $10 per year from a new customer for the next 10 years, the NPV for the customer, depending on the value of a dollar within your business, might be about $60.

▶ **Conversion ratio (overall).** This is the conversion ratio from someone clicking your AdWords ad (which costs you money) to that person buying from you (which brings in revenue and, hopefully, profit).

If each click costs you $1, and your profit per sale is $100, you need to convert at least 1% of your clickers into buyers to break even with AdWords. (Realistically, you need AdWords to consume only a share of your profits, not all of them.) It's okay to fall short of your profitability goals early on in your AdWords efforts, as you're learning, but making AdWords profitable should be your goal from day one.

Here's a somewhat complicated example. BATCS, which sells accent-reduction services in London, England, has two main products: In-person courses, which have a profit of about £100 for a sale averaging several hundred pounds, and a book, *Get Rid of Your Accent* (see Figure 7.2), which has a profit of about £5 for a sale averaging £20 at retail. AdWords ads contribute to both. For a total AdWords budget of £500 per month, BATCS has to realize at least five new students for the courses, 100 book sales, or a mix, for the ads to pay off.

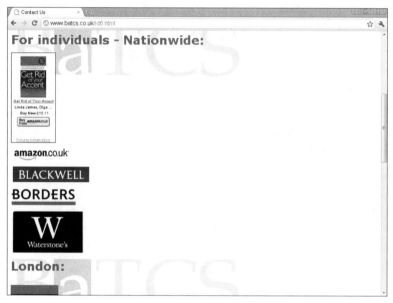

FIGURE 7.2   BATCS sells in-person courses and books.

AdWords offers two sets of bidding options: basic and advanced. (The advanced set of options, which includes the basic options discussed here, plus some additional ones, are shown in Figure 7.3.) The basic options are as follows:

▶ **Manual Bidding**. This option lets you set a maximum bid per keyword (which is set when you choose keywords, as described in Lesson 9, "Using Advanced Settings"). You have fine-tune control of your bidding.

▶ **Automatic Bidding**. AdWords adjusts your bid on each keyword to try to maximize clicks within your target budget.

What's the best option for you? It depends on your desired approach.

▶ If you have a good understanding of your sales pipeline and product profitability, and a good feel for AdWords and the amounts to bid for your needed keywords, you might want to use manual bidding right from the start. You'll quickly hone in on a good balance of bid amounts and profits made per click.

▶ If you don't really know the details, or you want to experiment, you might want to begin with automatic bidding. See where your average cost per click works out to be. Then work out whether you're making money from each keyword, based on its cost to you, and eliminate the ones that are costing you more than they're making you.

CAUTION: **Automatic Bidding**
Automatic bidding is convenient and a great learning tool, but it can be expensive. Consider using it only on an experimental basis, combined with careful analysis to eliminate keywords and bids that are unprofitable.

Using Advanced Bidding Options

Advanced bidding options are the same as the basic options, with some other choices. You won't have access to these options when creating a first campaign running on Google Search Network or the Search Network, for reasons described in this section. However, it's worth knowing what the advanced options are now, in case you want to change your campaign or create a new campaign that takes advantage of them.

The advanced options are shown, along with the other fields covered in this lesson, in Figure 7.3. Here are all the options available within the advanced options:

▶ **Focus on Clicks**. This is the default setting that's always used in the basic options. In the advanced options, the choice of **manual** or **automatic bidding**, described in the previous section, is available only if you choose the Focus on Clicks option.

FIGURE 7.3   Advanced bidding options can seem complex, but are powerful.

▶ **Use Conversion Tracking Data**. This option, available within the Focus on Clicks option, uses conversion tracking data to adjust your bids for keywords. Conversion tracking is described in Lesson 16, "Using Additional Reports and Tools."

▶ **Focus on Conversions**. This setting uses conversion tracking to help you manage the online sales pipeline all the way through to a sale, where one occurs. You have to set up conversion tracking to enable this, which is a complicated procedure, involving detailed interaction with your website, and is not covered in this book.

▶ **Focus on Impressions**. This option is only available when you run ads on the Content Network, described in Lesson 4, "Identifying Your Target Markets for AdWords." It helps optimize your campaign around getting your ad seen, rather than clicked.

The advanced options are confusing to new users and draw on knowledge and experience that you probably won't have until you first use cost-per-click bidding for a while, as described in this lesson. Consider using the basic options until you gain experience.

Setting a Daily Budget (Versus Monthly Spending)

After you choose how bidding works, as described in the previous sections in this lesson, it's time to set a budget. This could be the start of your making a lot of money—or spending a lot of money with little return.

You have to set a reasonably high budget to give your ads a chance to get established and develop a track record so that they get shown fairly often and have a chance to lead to both learning and sales for you. Unfortunately, the word *reasonably* here means, "reasonably" compared to the keywords you're advertising against, geographic breadth, and so on—not "reasonably" compared to what you can afford.

If you're in a fairly competitive business, such as selling shoes, you can expect intense competition for the relevant keywords. Narrowing the geographic area in which your ads are shown is a big help, but not a complete solution for the most popular keywords.

You could easily find yourself spending several dollars per click, but getting very few clicks—or many clicks, but few actual sales, if there are many competing options. You could spend a lot of money on AdWords before you even start to get results; or, if you keep your spending down, you might not get enough traction with your ads to get much use out of AdWords.

If, however, you sell a specialized brand of shoes, and advertise only in tightly defined local areas, you might well be able to get in the game—but only for the specific keywords that go with your shoes. You won't be picking up customers from people who search for *shoes*, but only from those who search for a specific brand name or unusually named characteristic of the shoes you sell.

Even for specialized, geographically targeted ads, you need to set a budget that might seem painfully high during the initial learning process. An amount such as $25 per day might at least start the learning curve (or, if your focus is narrow enough, actually might get you your first AdWords-based sales).

Of course, you don't want to spend $25 a day—that's about $750 a month on average, if you keep the same daily budget for that long—without knowing your results. So, when you start your AdWords campaign, be ready to use this book and the tools within AdWords to work hard to understand and improve the effectiveness of your ads.

> NOTE: **How AdWords Sets Monthly Budget Limits**
> AdWords doesn't completely respect your daily budget limit. It might go over the limit by as much as 20% on a given day. However, AdWords does use your daily budget limit to calculate a monthly limit, for months in which you keep your daily budget unchanged. (The monthly limit is your daily budget times 30.4, the average number of days in a month.) For instance, if your AdWords budget is $20 a day, your monthly limit will be $608. When AdWords exceeds your daily budget, you simply pay the extra, up to 20%. But when AdWords exceeds your monthly budget, you pay up to the limit only; any extra clicks that you get beyond your monthly budget are free.

Setting Position Preference and Delivery Method

Google offers you options for your position preference and delivery method. These are advanced options, shown in Figure 7.3. You access them by clicking the link that appears above them, Position Preference or Delivery Method (Advanced), or by clicking the + sign next to this link.

Position preference is a potentially valuable money-saving tool, and the delivery method can, in a pinch, help you avoid feeling like you're losing your mind.

The position preference is based on a simple observation: The top AdWords positions can cost a lot more than the middle-ranking ones, perhaps twice as much for many keywords. Yet the top position might not be twice as effective as a middle-ranking spot. So, you can get more showings and more clicks for your money by choosing to target certain placements besides the top ones.

This works best when you have an ad that is, for some reason, eye-catching and interesting to at least some users. Skip Frye is a famous surfer and surfboard shaper. An ad for a longboard with Skip Frye's name in it is likely to catch the eye of certain people even if it's not in the top position. So, you can specify that the ad never be shown in the top (most expensive) spots, meaning that it shows only when it would normally have appeared in a middle- or lower-ranking slot.

Now this does cut out some showings. In some cases, your ad might no longer get shown enough to spend your entire daily budget when you restrict the spots where it appears, so you have to manage this versus your needs and expectations. That's what makes it an advanced option.

If you turn on the Automatically Manage Maximum CPC Bids to Target a Preferred Position Range option, an additional field appears in the Keywords entry area. You fill this in to specify the desired range, as described in Lesson 9.

The delivery method is another advanced option—but it's the default method, the one that AdWords uses if you don't make a change, that seems both advanced and odd, whereas the "special" method, called Accelerated Delivery, seems more normal.

In the default—or Standard—method, AdWords attempts to spread showings of your ads throughout the day. That means that, if AdWords guesstimates that your ad would normally be shown 100 times a day, but your budget will only pay for about 50, Google displays your ad only every fourth time it would normally show up.

This drives people nuts. You go to a lot of work to get your AdWords campaign set up, and then wait the normal few hours that you have to wait for changes to show up on AdWords. Then you test the keywords you painstakingly chose to see if they cause your ad to show. Nothing. So you try again. Still nothing. Then you try one last time—and there it is! Your ad is being shown irregularly, just as AdWords intends.

The Accelerated option makes more intuitive sense. As soon as your ad is ready, it starts showing. It gets shown all day, unless it gets enough clicks to exhaust your daily budget for the day. If it does get the budgeted number of clicks, it stops showing.

For testing, you definitely want the Accelerated option so that you can quickly check whether the ad works as intended. For normal production ad campaigns, where the budget is too low to get you showings every time, it's up to you whether to spread the ad showings out or concentrate them earlier in the day.

> CAUTION: **When Your Ad Doesn't Show**
>
> When your ad doesn't show at times when you expect it to, check the delivery method. If it's on Standard, consider changing it to Accelerated while you test.

Setting Options for Bidding, Budget, and Delivery

Follow these steps to set options for bidding, budget, and delivery:

1. If you're not there already, go to AdWords and start creating a new campaign, as described in Lesson 5, "Setting Up a New Campaign." Choose the campaign type, give your campaign a name, and set the advertising networks and devices to run your ads on. Set the locations and languages, as well, as described in the previous lesson.

   You should be on the Campaigns tab, with the Bidding and Budget Campaign Settings area displayed.

2. Under the Bidding and Budget area, next to the Bidding option prompt, click the **Advanced Options** link, if you want to see advanced options (although you probably won't need them when you're just starting out). The options appear, as shown in Figure 7.3.

3. Choose **Manual Bidding** to set a maximum bid yourself for each keyword, or **Automatic Bidding** to let AdWords manage this within your budget. If you're using advanced options, refer to the earlier descriptions or use the onscreen help from Google to learn more.

> CAUTION: **Don't Overpay for Underperforming Keywords**
> Automatic bidding is a good way to let Google experiment for you,
> but watch carefully that you're not overpaying for keywords that
> don't turn into sales fast enough for you.

4. Enter the daily budget for your ad campaign, in the form 30.00,
   for example, for $30 a day.

> CAUTION: **Those Charges Add Up in a Hurry!**
> Your daily expenditure could exceed the budget by up to 20%.
> However, Google sets (and enforces) a monthly budget that's your
> daily budget times 30.4 if you don't change the daily budget in a
> given month. The charges can add up fast! Use the rest of this
> book to learn about AdWords quickly, so you're sure to get your
> money's worth from your daily expenditure.

5. Click the **Position Preference, Delivery Method (Advanced)**
   link. The Position preference and Delivery method options display.

6. To enable you to set the preferred position for your ad, change
   the Position preference to **On**. If you leave the setting to Off,
   Google shows ads as high up as your budget allows.

7. For Delivery Method, the Standard setting spaces your ads
   throughout the day. To show ads at every opportunity during the
   day, until your daily budget is exceeded, click **Accelerated** to
   change the setting.

   If you leave the setting to On, Google spaces the ads more or less
   evenly across the day.

8. To save the changes and continue to the next screen, click **Save
   and Continue**. For extensions to your ad and additional
   advanced settings, see the next lesson.

Summary

In this lesson, you learned how bids for search keywords work, and how strong ad copy helps your ad get shown more. You then learned how to set options for bidding for keywords, specifying your ad budget, and delivering your ads.

LESSON 8

Adding Extensions

In this lesson, you learn how to understand and use ad extensions. You also learn how to choose which extensions to use, and how to implement the Location, Product, Sitelinks, and Phone extensions.

Understanding Ad Extensions

A Google AdWords ad extension is additional relevant information that's shown along with your ad. Whether—and, if so, exactly when—you should use them is an open question.

The guiding principle behind information on the Internet often seems to be "too much is never enough." However, Google's search engine is famous for cutting through the clutter and getting straight to information that people really want. Your AdWords ad might benefit from a similar approach.

> NOTE: **More on Ad Extensions**
> To see more details and examples of ad extensions, click **Help** from within AdWords. A search window opens. Enter **ad extensions**. From the results, choose **Ad Extensions Formats Preview** for details of the appearance of each type of extension. For details on other aspects of extensions, choose another result.

Google's text ads are limited as to your budget of characters—each line is short, and the total number of characters in the ad is comparable to a text message or Twitter post. Yet these ads are successful.

Perhaps "less is more" is a good guiding principle. Begin by being selective in what information you consider including in your ad. Include only information that's directly relevant.

Then take advantage of AdWords to test whether extensions really help your ads perform better. Ad extensions are set at the level of a campaign, so consider creating a campaign with no ad extensions—then, in addition, a parallel campaign with all the same settings, but with relevant ad extensions turned on. You can then compare the results you get for each version.

What are sensible ad extensions? I invite you to take a look at the extensions, and what kind of advertising situations each might be best for:

▶ **Location**. The Location extension puts a link to a map on your ad. When the user clicks the link, a Google map appears, with your locations mapped out. An example of a Location extension is shown in Figure 8.1. Recommended.

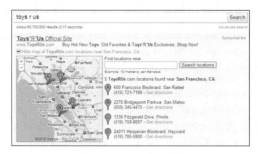

FIGURE 8.1   Location extensions help people find you.

▶ **Product**. Google has a Merchant Center that enables you to register your company and its products with Google. With the Product extension, a link appears on your ad. When the user clicks the link, a set of pictures and product names appears, with clickable links to the products. This is a lot of trouble, as it requires you to enter your company and products in the Google Merchant Center, so consider it carefully before using it.

▶ **Sitelinks**. Sitelinks extensions are detailed links to specific pages within your website. Sitelinks extensions appear as part of your ad. Sitelinks make your ad more powerful, but also more complex, so I can't strongly recommend for or against them.

▶ **Phone**. A Phone extension appears on mobile phones. It puts a clickable link to a phone number on your ad. This one's worthwhile because mobile users are often rushed and have many demands on their attention; giving them a clickable phone number makes it easy for them to act.

You will wonder, of course, what the costs for these extensions are. The good news is that, at this writing, they're free. That is, adding them to your ad is free, and—to a certain extent—so is using them.

However, that could change in the future. That makes it a good idea to experiment with extensions now, when you don't have to pay while you learn.

You still pay for clicks, though. You don't pay for clicks that merely open up information—for instance, when the user clicks the location ad extension and sees a map with your business location, that click is free. When the user clicks through to your website, though, you are charged.

Why would Google do this? Two reasons. First, the odds of the user clicking through—and paying Google—almost certainly go up with more information. Second, Google can always start charging extra for these features if they prove popular enough. It's a win-win for Google—and, as long as the extensions stay free, for you as well. Only if Google starts charging will you need to do a detailed cost-benefit analysis as to whether using the feature is worth it.

> TIP: **Try Extensions Now**
> With AdWords, as with other advertising, you have to experiment to see what works—and this usually costs you money, all the way through. With extensions, though, you can experiment for free. This is especially valuable if Google starts charging for using extensions later; if so, you'll be glad you experimented while they were still free.

If you're a beginning AdWords advertiser, you have to decide where to invest your time and energy. You want to have a successful AdWords campaign as soon as possible. That way, you start getting a return on the investment of time and money you're putting into AdWords. After you're successful in making AdWords profitable, you can build on your success.

Look at the different types of ad extensions, as described in the remainder of this lesson, and see which ones make the most sense to implement right away. For others, wait, or don't use that extension at all.

Using the Location Extension

For most businesses, the Location extension (shown in Figure 8.1) is really valuable. It ties your AdWords ad to your physical location. If you use geo-targeting (see Lesson 6, "Deciding Where to Show Your Ads,"), or Google Places (also mentioned in Lesson 6), using the Location extension is nearly a must.

The Location extension is also really valuable if you have multiple locations. The Location extension can be used with multiple locations; the closest one to the user appears in the ad. People want to be able to easily find the most convenient location for them to visit, whether that's near their home, the office, or on the way to and from various other destinations.

> NOTE: **Extensions and Mobile Devices**
>
> The Location extension and the Phone extension, described later in this lesson, are particularly pertinent to you for your customers who are using mobile devices. If you want to bring in customers who are using mobiles, which is the fastest-growing category of Internet use, seriously consider using these extensions.

There are some cases, though, where publicizing your location could be less helpful—or even a detriment. Examples of these instances include the following:

▶ **Internet businesses**. If you have a business based on a website, emphasizing your location is probably detrimental. You want anyone who can use the Internet, and who lives in the country or countries where you do business, to feel comfortable buying from you. Emphasizing a physical location would be counterproductive.

▶ **Small products with big distribution**. If you sell a product that's sold as a relatively small part of a bigger range of products—a book, a music album, or a can opener—you want to emphasize the type of place where your product is sold, not one particular outlet.

▶ **Advice-type businesses.** If you're a consultant giving advice, you might want to emphasize the region you're in, rather than your specific address. You want people to know that you are accessible within, say, the San Francisco Bay Area, not tie yourself to a particular city and neighborhood.

▶ **Some service businesses.** Like advice-type businesses, some service businesses are better off emphasizing their preferred area of operation rather than their physical address. This is especially true if the address is in an area known for being particularly rundown (a bad association) or especially affluent (people might think they'd just be making you richer).

Using the Product Extension

The Product extension, shown in Figure 8.2, is currently U.S.-only. It's really only useful if you already use Google Merchant Center, shown in Figure 8.3, or plan to. This is a fair amount of work, so consider your needs carefully before using the Product extension.

FIGURE 8.2   The Product extension can be eye-catching.

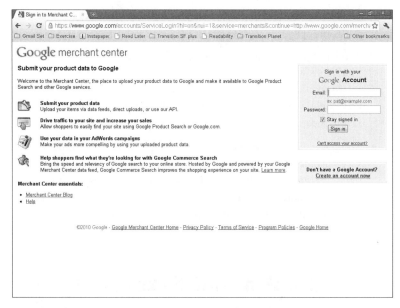

FIGURE 8.3   The Google Merchant Center is a good support site for online sales and AdWords ads.

If you already have products on Google Merchant Center, using the Product extension for at least some of your ads is almost certainly worthwhile. But what if you don't; should you go to the trouble to do so?

The answer, if your business is product centric, is probably yes. The combination of AdWords ads and the Product extension enables you to pack much of the power of a website into AdWords ads that appear in Google search and elsewhere.

The combination of Google Merchant Center and AdWords works best if you have products that meet certain criteria:

- ▶ **Sold online**. Users can quickly fulfill their desire for your product if both the initial impression (via AdWords and the Product extension) and the opportunity to buy are online. This is true whether the product is also available from you by other means, such as in a shop or by phone or mail order.

▶ **Easily understood.** People searching are looking for quick hits of information. If your product is easily understood—or if some aspect of its appeal can be quickly conveyed—it will be more AdWords friendly.

▶ **Looks good in photos.** Your product will benefit if it has an eye-candy aspect such that it looks good in images. Of course, a lot of that is down to taking a good photo, and then making it into an online-friendly image.

Think through how your product will look and work online as something to attract people's attention through a quick hit of information. If you're in doubt, go ahead. You can learn an awful lot about your products and how to sell them better by experimenting with them in AdWords.

If you do decide to go ahead, the only question is timing. Getting your products into Google Merchant Center is likely to be a fair amount of work. You're already starting with AdWords now—and it might be worth getting going with AdWords first, and then getting your products in the Google Merchant Center and using the product extension.

> TIP: **Save Money Early**
>
> Should you go ahead with AdWords first, with the intention of using Google Merchant Center and the Product extension later, keep your initial spending low; concentrate on learning AdWords well. That way you have some gold in your treasure chest for further experimentation when your products are ready to add to your AdWords ad. (Try saying that three times fast!)

Using Ad Sitelinks

Ad Sitelinks are additional links into your website that show as part of your AdWords ad. An example of Sitelinks is shown in Figure 8.4.

Sitelinks are, for the most part, a good thing. They add depth and value to your ad. They might also make it more likely that the user will click a link that they find immediately useful, and therefore will be more likely to do business with you.

FIGURE 8.4   Sitelinks give your AdWords ads multiple entry points for users.

However, Sitelinks are not an unalloyed positive. There are several concerns, as well:

▶ **Sitelinks add complexity and choice**. Much of the advantage of AdWords is that ads are small and focused; clicks can occur almost reflexively. With Sitelinks, your ads are more complex and require more attention.

▶ **Sitelinks demand good landing pages**. Your AdWords ad should have a good landing page, as described in Lesson 15, "Using Opportunities and Improving Landing Pages." For every Sitelinks link, though, you need a separate, optimized landing page.

▶ **You're not in full control**. When you add links via Sitelinks, you can add up to 10 links. However, not all of them will get displayed every time. Only the top-ranked AdWords ad gets Sitelinks displayed at all. Then, the higher the quality of your ad, the more likely that some or all of your Sitelinks will be displayed; no guarantees!

▶ **Extra effort for you.** The fact that Sitelinks display is unreliable means extra effort and checking by you to see what's going on and to understand the results you get (or don't get).

CAUTION: **Sitelinks Might Not Always Work**

Sitelinks might not be the best thing for every AdWords campaign. For one thing, only the top-ranked ad for a given search displays Sitelinks. Carefully consider your options before using Sitelinks in a given campaign.

Given that Sitelinks are extra work for everyone involved, I suggest that you first create and run your ad campaign without Sitelinks. Then create a separate, similar campaign with them. Compare the results to see how much value the Sitelinks extension adds.

Using Phone Extensions

Phone extensions are the simplest type of extension, the most limited in their application (for now), and the most obvious type to go ahead and use.

A Phone extension simply lists the phone number that users can call when they view your AdWords ad on a mobile device that supports a full web browser. The user can simply touch the number to make a call.

This makes excellent sense for mobile users, who are, by definition, on the move. They might be harried, hurried, and harassed. Being able to get in touch with you by a single click makes a lot of sense.

In fact, in many cases, it makes a lot more sense than having the same user click a link to go to a website on her mobile device. This is especially true if the website in question isn't optimized for use on a mobile, with its small screens and often-slow connection speeds.

Although it's certainly possible to have a mobile-optimized site, it's a lot of work that you might not want to go through right away. You're probably better off optimizing your current site first, especially for use with AdWords.

Speaking of optimizing your site, there is a kind of optimization that's especially important for AdWords and use of the Phone extension. That's getting your ad into one of the top few places, or even *the* top place, in the ad rankings. Why?

Because mobile screens are so small, they don't show much content in every screen. Figure 8.5 is an example, from a Google Nexus One phone. Now this phone is relatively high resolution, but as you can see, not much shows up on the first screen of results. (In fact, the figure shows the bottom of the first page of results, after scrolling down by several screens. Not many users would be likely to make it that far.)

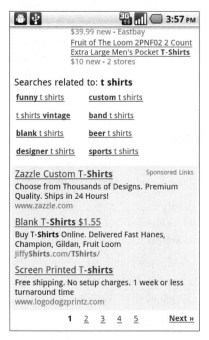

FIGURE 8.5 Only a few search results and ads fit on a crowded mobile phone screen.

So, if your ad doesn't show up in the first few AdWords results, it's unlikely to get noticed. You probably won't get much of a result from the Phone extension if you're not there. By all means, set up the Phone extension—then use the information in this book to create great ads (as described in Lesson 11, "Finding Your Keywords") tied to the right keywords (see Lesson 12, "Choosing Placements and Bids") that get good results (see Lesson 14, "Updating Your Campaign").

Setting Ad Extensions

Follow these steps to set ad extensions:

1. If you're not there already, go to AdWords and start creating a new campaign, as described in Lesson 5, "Setting Up a New Campaign." From the Campaigns tab, choose the campaign type, give your campaign a name, and set the advertising networks and devices to run your ads on. Set the locations and languages, as well, as described in Lesson 6, "Deciding Where to Show Your Ads," and your bidding options and budget, as described in Lesson 7, "Setting Your Bidding, Budget, and Delivery Options."

You should be on the Campaigns tab, with the Ad Extensions and Advanced Settings areas displayed.

2. For Location, click the check box to turn on the Location extension.

You are given two options:

▶ To use addresses from a Google Places account, if you have one, or

▶ To use manually entered addresses

3. To get addresses from a Google Places account, check the check box. Specify the Google Places account you want to use, and choose or upload a map icon.

You are given two options:

▶ To use addresses from a Google Places account, if you have one, or

▶ To use manually entered addresses.

TIP: **Addresses for the Location Extension**

You can use addresses from Google Places in addition to manually entered addresses. Just check both check boxes and enter the relevant information for each.

4. To enter addresses manually, check the check box, as shown in
   Figure 8.6. Enter the address information and choose or upload a
   map icon. Optionally, choose or upload an image to represent
   your business.

FIGURE 8.6   Enter addresses for your locations.

5. If you use Google Merchant Center, you can add product details
   from it. Click the check box and follow the instructions onscreen.

NOTE: **Google Merchant Center**

Adding product details from Google Merchant Center is not covered
in detail here because it requires you to have a Google Merchant
Center account and product listings, which most people won't have.
If you want to learn more about Google Merchant Center, see http:
//www.google.com/support/merchants/.

6. To add Sitelinks, click the check box. Add up to 10 links (text and link URL).

   Your Sitelinks will be shown with your ad only when it's the top-ranked ad for a given search. The higher the quality of your top-ranked ad, the more Sitelinks will be shown. However, you should include only the best Sitelinks to avoid distracting the user away from the good ones.

7. To add a phone number, click the check box. Enter your country and your phone number.

8. If you are done with the page, or if you want to save your entries so far, click the **Save and Continue** button. Or, if you prefer, continue to the Advanced Settings area, as described in the next lesson.

Summary

In this lesson, you learned how to understand and use ad extensions. You also learned how to choose which extensions to use, and how to implement the Location, Product, Sitelinks, and Phone extensions.

LESSON 9
Using Advanced Settings

In this lesson, you learn how and when to use advanced settings, including start and end dates; day and time scheduling by weekday; ad rotation; and, for the Display Network only, frequency capping and demographic bidding. You also learn how to set each of the options.

Using the Schedule Advanced Setting

The advanced settings—Schedule, Ad Delivery, and Demographic Bidding—are shown in Figure 9.1. (Detailed settings for time-of-day and day-of-week scheduling, and for demographic bidding, are shown separately later in this lesson.)

Schedule options include two very different kinds of options. The first is highly recommended: start and end dates for your campaign. The start date is initially set to the date you create the campaign. However, you can set it to some future date, and your campaign won't start running until then.

Using the end date is an especially good idea. With AdWords, it's all too easy to keep running a losing campaign, or even just a campaign that's simply not optimized. By putting in an end date, you provide closure, and give yourself and, if you choose, others, the opportunity to evaluate what's happened so far, look for improvements, and proceed with the advertising only after you've implemented those improvements.

FIGURE 9.1   You can control the fine points of your ad display.

Combining the two—start date and end date—enables you to create campaigns that align cleanly with real-world events, such as the initial launch period for a new product, or with the calendar, as with a campaign that lasts exactly one month. Using dates in this way adds rigor and safety (from wasting money on a suboptimal campaign) to your AdWords work.

Ad scheduling for days of the week and times of day is a lot more complex, and a lot more fun. Figure 9.2 shows the ad scheduling options.

You can control when your ads appear, by day of week and time, literally down to the hour. But why would you use this feature?

There are two reasons. The first is to avoid periods when your target audience is unlikely to be at the computer. If your company sells to students, for example, you might want to prevent your ads from showing between mid-morning through to late afternoon. That way you can avoid showing your ads when most of your target audience is in school, and display it only when they're likely to be home and online.

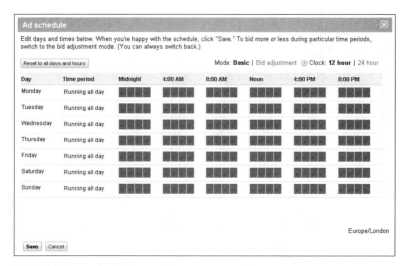

FIGURE 9.2   You can improve day and time options endlessly.

> CAUTION: **Time Keeps Ticking**
>
> It's easy to spend a great deal of time messing with date and time options. Keep changes few, and make them at some sensible, memorable time—the beginning of the week, for instance—to enhance your ability to compare periods and find out what really works for you.

The second is to optimize the showing of your ads. Just for example, let's say you run a coffee shop. You might want to show your ads early in the morning only, at least at first, because you know that coffee shop attendance peaks in a couple of hours in the morning.

This doesn't mean that you'll never advertise at other times of day. However, it's best to start with your strengths and get the most bang for your buck. After you establish profitability with a campaign that's limited in time, you can gradually extend it, checking for continued profitability the whole way through.

> TIP: **Keep Your Notes**
>
> Keep careful records of which scheduling options you're using when. That way, you can make needed adjustments to the data when comparing one period to another.

Using the Ad Delivery Advanced Setting

Ad delivery options, shown earlier in Figure 9.1, enable you to use your "best players" more often—and to optimize your use of the Display Network, if you choose to enable it.

The option that helps to run your best ads is Ad rotation. There are two choices:

- ▶ **Optimize.** This option is the default. It shows better-performing ads more often than poorer-performing ones. With this setting, you get more bang for your buck—although you might not get enough showings of poorer-performing ads to be sure that it's time to pull them.

- ▶ **Rotate.** This option shows ads more or less evenly. Even ads with a lower click-through rate or Quality Score will keep appearing frequently. It's up to you to pull or modify poorer-performing ads.

On balance, it's probably better to use the Optimize option. This allows for a kind of Darwinian survival of the fittest that helps you get more for your AdWords buck.

The other option for ad delivery is Frequency Capping. This option applies to only the Display Network; that is, ads on websites that have chosen to use AdSource to get AdWords ads on their site. (If that doesn't make sense, try saying it three times fast.)

You can cap the number of times a given user sees your ad. You can set the limit to a number you choose—to a number per day, per week, or per month—and you can do it within a campaign, within an ad group, or for a specific ad. That is, you can ensure that a given user only sees any ad from your campaign once, or only from an ad group, or only a specific ad.

However, none of this is perfect. Google can identify specific machines most of the time, and specific users who sign in to their Google accounts, but there's plenty of room for error. Google, though, is highly motivated to keep improving this and other aspects of AdWords.

NOTE: **Frequency Capping**

It might make sense to limit the frequency with which any one user sees any ad from you to once per—well, forever. But research shows that users often need to see an ad many times before their odds of acting on it start to rise. (I was once involved in some testing for an ad that needed three viewings before it got any traction.) So, use frequency capping to stop excessive showings per user, but not to prevent any and all repetition.

Using the Demographic Bidding Advanced Setting

Demographic bidding is a way for you to play with the big boys—that is, with pros who make television advertising buys, for instance, to reach specific audiences, such as young, presumably beer-drinking males in their 20s.

NOTE: **Content Network Only**

As with frequency capping, described in the previous section, demographic bidding works only on the Content Network, not the Search Network. Unlike frequency capping, demographic bidding is available on only certain sites that retain demographic data, so it's not effective on all sites. Because of this uncertainty, don't count on it to make a huge difference unless you limit the sites you advertise on to those that support demographic bidding.

Demographic bidding, shown in Figure 9.3, gives you many options:

▶ **Male/Female Exclusion or Bidding**. You can exclude males or females from your ad displays or increase the bid for one group or the other. (You can't increase the bid used by a group you've excluded, and increasing the bid for both groups doesn't make much sense because one increase just partly offset the other.)

▶ **Age Group Exclusion or Bidding**. You can exclude specific age groups from your ad displays, or increase the bid for one group or another. As with gender, you can't increase the bid used by a group you've excluded, but it does make sense to modify more than one age group bid—as long as at least one age group remains unmodified.

► **Combined exclusion or bidding.** You can exclude or make bid changes to both male-female groups and age groups. You can think of males and females as two rows, and of age groups as columns, in a grid. Bid modifications are additive, although any exclusions eliminate the effects of bid modifications.

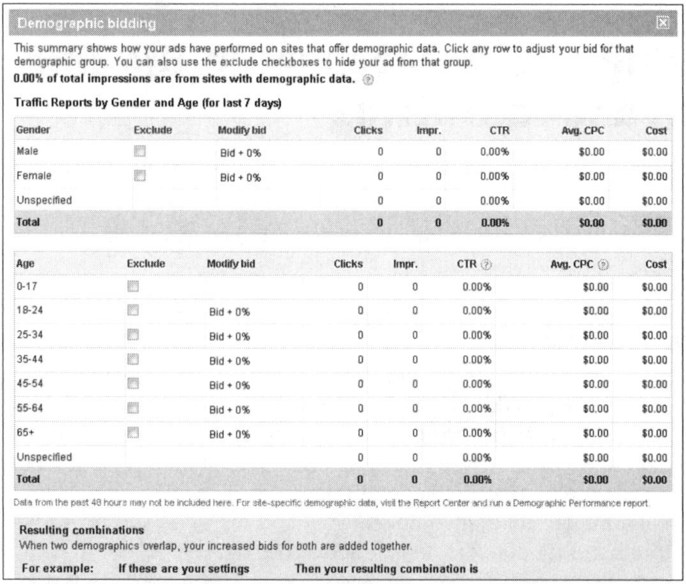

FIGURE 9.3 Demographic bidding helps you work hard for clicks.

You can use any of seven age ranges:

► **0-17.** Kids, "tweens" (roughly 10- to 12-year-olds), and teenagers.

► **18-24** and **24-34.** Young adults, "Gen Y"—people who grew up with computers in the home and in schools.

► **35-44** and **45-54.** Middle-aged people, currently including Generation X (born 1965–1984) and the younger Baby Boomers (born 1945–1964).

► **55-64** and **65+**. The bulk of the Baby Boomers and the Greatest Generation, those who survived the Great Depression and fought World War II.

Setting Advanced Settings

Follow these steps to set extensions and advanced settings:

1. If you're not there already, go to AdWords and start creating a new campaign, as described in Lesson 5, "Setting Up a New Campaign." Choose the campaign type, give your campaign a name, and set the locations and languages, as described in Lesson 6, "Deciding Where to Show Your Ads." Set the advertising networks and devices to run your ads on as well, and set your bidding options and budget, as described in the previous lesson.

   You should be on the Campaigns tab, with the Ad Extensions and Advanced Settings areas displayed.

2. For ad extensions, click to set or clear the options described in Lesson 8, "Adding Extensions": **Location, Product, Sitelinks**, or **Phone**.

   Note that Product links will work only if you enter your company and products in the Google Merchant Center. If you have multiple locations, the phone number in your Location extension information is store-specific, whereas the Phone extension is better-suited to a number used on multiple sites, such as a hotel chain. See details on extensions in the previous lesson.

3. For Schedule, if you so choose, enter the start/end date for your campaign.

4. Also for Schedule, next to Ad Scheduling, click the **Edit** link to change the days and hours shown. The Ad Schedule dialog appears—it's shown, without any changes to the schedule, as you saw earlier in Figure 8.3. Ad scheduling is not available with automatic bidding.

5. To change the hours for a day, click **Running All Day**, or specific hours, under the Time Period column header.

    A dialog appears, as shown in Figure 9.4, that enables you to change the time period that the ad is running, add other time periods for the ad to run, or set the ad to not run that day at all. You can also use the Copy pull-down to copy the schedule to all seven days or only to the weekdays, click **OK** when you are done. Then click **Save** to exit the Ad schedule dialog.

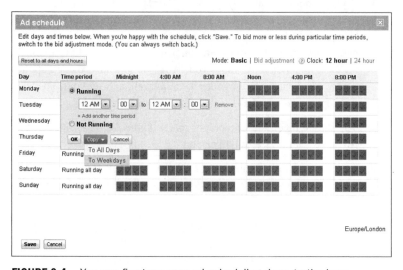

FIGURE 9.4   You can fine-tune your ad scheduling down to the hour.

6. For the ad rotation, choose a radio button to optimize the campaign around better-performing ads, or to rotate the showings evenly across ads regardless of performance.

7. To specify frequency capping (Content Network only), choose the appropriate radio button, and then enter the number of impressions, the time period for the limit (per day, per week, or per month), and whether the limitation is for an entire campaign, per ad group, or per ad.

8. To specify demographic bidding (Content Network only), click the **Edit** link. Then specify male-female and age group exclusions or additional bidding percentages. Click **Save** when you have finished.

9. To save the changes and continue to the next screen, click **Save and Continue**.

Summary

In this lesson, you learned how and when to use advanced settings, including start and end dates; day and time scheduling by weekday; ad rotation; and, for the Display Network only, frequency capping and demographic bidding. You also learned how to set each of the options.

LESSON 10

Writing Great Ads

In this lesson, you learn how ads work to help you do more business, how the lines within a text ad work together, and how to write an ad that gets results. You also learn about the various types of ads that AdWords offers, and the strengths and weaknesses of each, as well as how to create a text ad, step by step.

Understanding What Ads Do

Your AdWords ad is one of the crucial links in a chain between a user's search and you making a sale. Here's the big picture:

- ▶ **Keywords.** Users search on certain keywords that you bid for (see Lesson 11, "Finding Your Keywords"). If your bid for that keyword is high enough, and your ad is getting enough clicks, the user sees your ad.

- ▶ **Ads.** The user sees your ad. If he decides to click it, you're charged—a price at, or somewhat lower than, your bid. (You're actually charged one penny more than the next bid lower than yours.) If your ad gets more clicks, AdWords gives it more weight in deciding which ads to show against your chosen keywords.

- ▶ **Landing page.** The user goes to your landing page. The higher the traffic and links to your landing page, the more weight Google gives your ad.

- ▶ **Purchase.** Your landing page should help convert people who click your ad into your paying customers.

To focus in on the ad, it has just one key purpose: as part of the conversion chain between keywords being entered and you getting a customer.

However, there are two kinds of conversion here: narrow and broad. The narrow conversion is from looking to clicking—the user sees your ad and clicks it. This is the conversion rate for the ad. You get charged, and Google gets paid.

Google rewards your ad for these clicks. The more clicks your ad gets, the more weight Google gives it in deciding which ads to show against certain keywords. You can even save money this way. Even if you bid less on a keyword, your ad can still get shown—and shown higher—if it's proven to get lots of clicks.

Why? Because Google cares how much money it makes. And Google gets paid for clicks—a high keyword bid that results in few clicks does Google little good. A lower keyword bid that gets more clicks results in more total money for Google. (It also means more benefit for the user, but Google might or might not weight that highly.)

There's a problem here, though. Google gets paid for clicks. You get "paid"—that is, make any money—only when the user actually follows through and becomes your customer.

The machinery of AdWords encourages you to choose the right keywords, bid high on them, write great ads, and get clicks—and therefore to spend more money with Google. However, although Google will help, it's up to you to get from spending money (by getting clicks) to making money (by getting sales).

The way you write your ad can help a lot here. You want to discourage wastage—which in this context means people clicking your ad, but not buying from you.

So, your ad has to not only get clicks—it has to get clicks from people who are likely buyers from you. Here's the big picture for encouraging clickers who are more likely to become buyers:

- ▶ **Keyword selection**. You have to choose keywords that work not just for getting clicks, but for buying *your* specific products and services (see Lesson 11). For instance, if you're selling footballs, you want keywords that relate to *playing* football rather than *watching* football.

▶ **Ad text**. Your ad text shouldn't just get clicks—it should point toward a purchase. Again, if you're selling footballs, write ad text that attracts clicks from football players (however occasional and amateur), not football watchers.

▶ **Landing page**. After users reach your landing page, you've paid for them to get there. Your landing page should do everything possible to get something in return—if not a purchase then and there, then information for follow-up marketing.

▶ **Purchase**. Make sure to eliminate any and all barriers between the user arriving at your landing page and actually buying something from you.

So, the ad text has a lot of work to do—encouraging the right kind of clicks, that lead to a purchase from you, and discouraging the wrong kind, that lead to disappointment (that is, no purchase) for the user as well as you.

Writing a Great Ad

An AdWords ad has three lines, plus a displayed URL and a destination URL:

▶ **Headline (clickable) – "Click me."** The headline is 25 characters long, about four words. The headline describes what you offer. It's short, clickable, and on top of the ad, so it jumps out at the reader. It's an appeal; its function is to say "click me" to the (right kind of) user. Violent imagery and odd punctuation don't do the job here. What works is simple, descriptive text, preferably including the keyword the user searched with.

▶ **Description line 1 – "Details."** Both lines of the description are 35 characters long, about six words. Although the first line can be anything you want, it typically is true description, filling out the appeal contained in the headline. The function is "hygiene"— reassuring users that the ad is likely to be for something that will truly meet their needs.

▶ **Description line 2 – "Urgency."** Like the first line of the
description, this one is also 35 characters, about six words. The
second line of the description can also be anything you want, but
the usual purpose of this line is to create urgency about clicking.
Urgency can be created by many kinds of appeals, but a discount,
other kind of special offer, or some kind of time limitation are
the usual tools. In keeping with the urgency theme, the second
line is often quite short.

▶ **Display URL.** This is the URL that gets shown to the user. It
should be of two types: Your main site URL, to orient the user
to the site they're going to if they click your ad; or, the main
URL plus a subdomain, to reinforce the specific offer the user is
pursuing.

▶ **Destination URL.** This is the landing page that the user goes to
after clicking your ad. It should be specific to the product or service being advertised—or, better yet, to the ad campaign or ad
that the user is responding to. That way the page can be customized to continue the user's momentum all the way through to
a purchase.

Let's look at a couple of examples for BATCS—one to promote the
courses it offers; another to promote the book it sells.

Writing an Ad for a Course

The first example ad I show you is for a course to reduce one's accent. In
the United Kingdom, many people want to have an accent that's called
received pronunciation, as used by the Queen, people in the media, and
others who are accomplished and in visible positions. This accent is common in London and the heavily populated Southeast, but many Brits speak
with stronger or weaker regional accents. Foreigners, of course, are likely
to have accents of their own—and to want to sound more British, for com-
prehensibility and to get ahead in their careers.

> **NOTE: Online-Offline Conversion**
>
> Using an online ad to sell a course such as the accent-reduction course offered by BATCS is a bit tricky. That's because there's an online-to-offline step in the overall conversion process: The user is attracted by the AdWords ad, which of course is online, but then has to make a phone call to get information and show up in person for evaluation and to make payment. This process is so complicated that it's worthwhile only because of the low cost-per-click of the ad (about £1) and the high price of the course (about £500). BATCS pays about £500 a month in AdWords costs to get an average of four students a month, which is worthwhile, but not a huge win.

The home page of BATCS, featuring the accent-reduction courses, is shown in Figure 10.1. This is where users will go if they click the ad.

FIGURE 10.1 BATCS offers courses to help reduce one's accent.

Here's an example of an ad for BATCS, showing the character counts for each line:

Accent reduction course (23 characters)
Experienced teacher; London location (33 characters)
Course starts 20th October (23 characters)
www.batcs.co.uk

This ad does the job well, at least as far as one can tell before running it. The text fills the budget of characters allowed for the first two lines. The third line is shorter and to the point, inviting the user to click now. Here's a line-by-line breakdown:

- ► **Headline.** Text: "Accent reduction course." The headline is descriptive: If you want to reduce your accent, here's a course for you.

- ► **Description line 1.** Text: "Experienced teacher; London location." The second line gives relevant details to support the offer in the headline: The teacher is experienced, and the location is in London, the United Kingdom's largest city (also the one with by far the most immigrants, whether from other countries or other parts of the United Kingdom, where people have regional accents they might want to lose).

  The "London location" indicator also plays a vital role in reducing clicks from people outside London, so they don't generate expense for the advertiser (from the clicks) without concomitant revenue (because they're unlikely to follow through and take the course if they live far away). If there were room for only one descriptive phrase—"experienced teacher" or "London location"—it's the second one that would be kept.

- ► **Description line 2.** Text: "Course starts 20th October." The third line imparts urgency without giving away any revenue: The course start date is a natural deadline. This line could also be rewritten as "course starts in 7 days," for example, to be more urgent. The trade-off is that the ad would then need to be updated every day to reflect the countdown to the actual course start date.

▶ **Display URL**. Text: "www.batcs.co.uk." The display URL is easy, in this case—it's the home page, which is also the landing page for the ad.

It's a good idea to include your keywords in ad text that you write, so this ad would work well with keywords such as "accent," "accent reduction," "accent course," and similar.

Writing an Ad for Online Book Sales

Let's look at a second example for BATCS, one that promotes the book it sells, *Get Rid of Your Accent*. The book is very popular in U.K. bookshops and on the country's version of Amazon, which is at the URL http://www.amazon.co.uk.

Figure 10.2 shows the Amazon page for the book. This is where users go if they click the ad and then follow on from the landing page.

FIGURE 10.2 Amazon users like *Get Rid of Your Accent*.

Here's the second ad:

Get Rid of Your Accent (22 characters)
Book with two CDs of examples (29 characters)
Only £16.95 today – £3 discount (31 characters)
www.batcs.co.uk/book

> NOTE: **Supply Chains and Profits**
>
> Many of the book sales generated by the ad shown here are completed on Amazon, so the conversion process is all online.
> However, the profit picture is not quite so pretty. The book is sold into a distributor at a standard 40% discount, and the distributor supplies both bookstores and Amazon. So, the sales generated by the ad have to pay for the profit not only of the advertiser, BATCS, but also the distributor and Amazon.

This ad is a bit less satisfying because there are a lot of things that could be said but that don't fit within the space constraints—yet the chosen phrases, although informative, don't fill the budget of characters allowed. The offer in the third line is a bit confusing. Here's a line-by-line breakdown:

- ▶ **Headline**. Text: "Get Rid of Your Accent." The headline is simply the book title. It would be great to get the word "book" in there, too, to help select potential buyers for clicking the ad; unfortunately, that would make the headline two characters too long, and the book title can't easily be abbreviated.

- ▶ **Description line 1**. Text: "Book with two CDs of examples." Accent-reduction books distinguish themselves by the number of CDs they have. *Get Rid of Your Accent* is the lowest-priced title of its type with any CDs at all, and reader feedback has indicated that having two CDs is "just right"—enough to be credible, not so many as to be intimidating. So, this line does a great job of supporting the headline.

- ▶ **Description line 2**. Text: "Only £16.95 today – £3 discount." The third line offers a low price and a discount. The word "today" is a somewhat weak attempt to indicate urgency because there's no actual deadline.

▶ **Display URL**. Text: "www.batcs.co.uk/book." The display URL gives the main URL along with a specific focus on the book. The actual landing page URL could be different.

What keywords would work well with this ad? "Accent," "accent reduction," "accent book," and similar keywords would work well. For other keywords, the ad text could be tweaked, where possible, to include the keyword.

Choosing Different Types of Ads

Text ads are the basis of almost all AdWords advertising campaigns. They're simple, effective, easy to display widely, and enable you to test all sorts of concepts quickly and easily. So, unless you're an expert in using images or multimedia ads, you should use text ads as the main focus of your AdWords advertising.

AdWords does, though, offer several other types of ads. Because they're so different, and not likely to be used by most AdWords advertisers, I just describe them briefly here. If one or more of these types of ads is of interest to you, consider doing everything you can to create and launch a successful AdWords campaign based on text ads. Then, when you've achieved at least initial success, consider adding other kinds of ads to your mix.

Following are descriptions of the alternatives for your ad types that you can use in AdWords—except text ads, which are covered in detail in this lesson.

Image Ads

Image ads are made in certain sizes considered standard for online advertising. Examples are available in AdWords, as shown in Figure 10.3.

Image ads have so many possibilities that it can be mind-boggling just to consider them, let alone to decide on the ad, create it, test it, and then do the whole thing again. This extra work can be overwhelming for a small advertiser, when the potential benefit is compared to the time and cost involved.

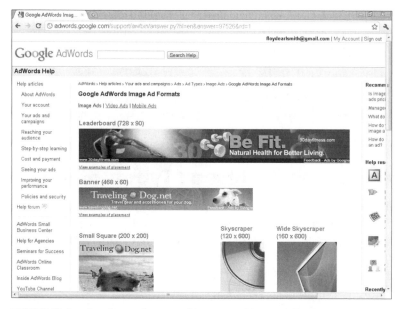

FIGURE 10.3   Google supports a wide range of image ad types.

The best case for using image ads in AdWords is if you already have the *creative*—the ad or ads, with images and words—from other online ad campaigns. Then your only costs for AdWords are for actually running the ad.

Conversely, if you're considering creating new image ads for use in AdWords, consider reusing the creative in other online advertising campaigns.

The best image ads for AdWords include the keywords you use in the text, as well as the URL of the site that the user visits, and use simple, appealing images. Repurposing a successful text ad is a great way to seed the creative process for an image ad.

> **TIP: Base Image Ads on Text Ads**
>
> Plan to spend a lot of time testing and evaluating your "creative," as the pros call the contents of ads, as well as the actual campaign, and its high and low points. The effort involved is probably worthwhile only if you're already making hundreds or thousands of dollars in profit a month from your AdWords text ads.

Display Ads

Display ads are inserted into audio and video displays from Google, such as YouTube ads. Display ads have a variety of formats. For instance, moving or static images, or audio clips, can be inserted into YouTube clips and other multimedia content. Figure 10.4 shows some of the ad formats you can use.

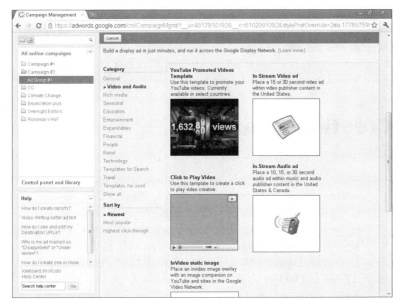

FIGURE 10.4   Google can support still, video, and audio ads within media streams.

Although display ads have tremendous potential, creating, deploying, and tracking them is a big issue. This is a relatively new field, so there might not yet be content out there that's a good home for your ad. Many of the most popular clips on YouTube, for example, are silly things such as skateboarding dogs; only certain kinds of products and accompanying creative are really friendly to this kind of container.

As with other specialized kinds of ads, the best case for using display ads is as a way to extend the use of creative that you already have on hand from other advertising efforts. Even so, be ready for a lot of hassle compared to the initial benefits, and undertake this kind of effort only if you're already having good success with other AdWords advertising efforts.

WAP Mobile Ads

Smart phones, such as the iPhone and Android phones, can show regular AdWords text ads. So, a WAP mobile ad is one that displays on a "dumb phone"—of which there are hundreds of millions, so this is not a bad target market. However, you want to be somewhat of an AdWords expert before you undertake this specialized kind of advertising.

With mobile ads, users who click are sent to your mobile web page, which you also have to create and maintain. Create mobile ads in a separate campaign so that you can manage and measure the results effectively. Although you might struggle at first, the use of mobile advertising is growing rapidly, so your results may in turn improve over time as well.

Creating a Text Ad

Follow these steps to create a text ad:

1. If you're not there already, go to AdWords and start creating a new campaign, as described in Lesson 5, "Setting Up a New Campaign." Choose the campaign type, give your campaign a name, and set the advertising networks and devices to run your ads on. Set the locations and languages, as well, as described in Lesson 6, "Deciding Where to Show Your Ads;" your bidding options and budget, as described in Lesson 7, "Setting Your Bidding, Budget, and Delivery Options;" and your extensions and advanced settings, as described in Lessons 8, "Adding Extensions," and 9, "Using Advanced Settings." If you are using AdWords for the very first time, you'll need to click **Save and continue**.

   You should be on the Campaigns tab, with the Create Ad Group area displayed, as shown in Figure 10.5. (If you're using AdWords for the very first time, the tab shows Create Ad and keywords.)

2. If requested, enter the ad group name (up to 255 characters).

   The name should represent whatever's distinctive about this ad group; for instance, if it's for a specific type of ad such as an

image ad, you might want to name it "Book – Image ad – Mt
Rushmore." You can only count on about 25 characters displaying in some views of the ad group name, so keep it short. (The
example is 29 characters.)

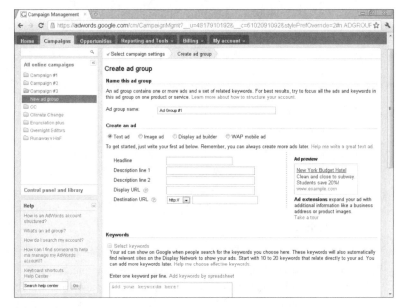

FIGURE 10.5   AdWords displays your ad as you build it up.

3. Enter the headline (up to 25 characters).

Enter the headline for your ad. It should be simple, descriptive,
and eye-catching, but without resorting to gimmicks such as ALL
CAPS, UnUsUaL capitalization, or <<<Using special charac-
ters>>>. AdWords rejects many such attempts when you go to
save the ad group, but they're a bad idea even if you can get
away with them.

4. Enter the description line 1 (up to 35 characters).

The first line of description should support the headline. Its main
purpose is to reassure the users that key details that they care
about are indeed correct. For instance, if you're selling galoshes,

and the only color is black, say so: "Best prices on all-black galoshes." That way you get clicks only from people who indeed want black galoshes, preserving your AdWords dollars and avoiding wasting your users' time.

5. Enter the description line 2 (up to 35 characters).

The second line of description should include some kind of special offer, deadline, or other kind of attraction or urgency. You should also consider keeping it shorter than even the allotted 35-character space so that users can finish reading the ad and get on with clicking the headline.

6. Enter the display URL.

Enter the display URL, which the user sees as part of the ad. Consider entering only the home page URL, such as www.batcs.co.uk, or the home page URL plus a subdirectory relevant to the ad's focus, such as www.batcs.co.uk/book.

7. Enter the destination URL.

Enter the URL of the page you want the users to reach when they click the headline. This can be the main page of your site, a specific page inside your site, or a customized landing page created just for this purpose.

Summary

In this lesson, you learned how ads work to help you do more business, how the lines within a text ad work together, and how to write an ad that gets results. You also learned about the various types of ads that AdWords offers, and the strengths and weaknesses of each, as well as how to create a text ad, step by step.

LESSON 11

Finding Your Keywords

In this lesson, you learn how to generate keywords from the bottom up, based on the products and services you sell, as well as how to adjust your ads to reflect keywords. You are then shown keyword tools and techniques for specifying different types of keywords, as well as how to enter keywords and key phrases for your campaign, generating cost and search traffic estimates along the way.

Tying Keywords to What You Sell

The basic mechanism of AdWords is to tie the keywords that users are typing in to the words that describe whatever you're selling. You want to use not only the keywords that bring people to your ad, though. You want the ones that will lead people to click your ad, over others, and to buy from you.

There are two approaches to keywords, only one of which I recommend you use:

▶ **Top-down approach.** This approach starts with people who are searching. You find out what the most popular keywords are and try to tie those to what you're selling.

▶ **Bottom-up approach.** This approach starts with you and what you're offering. You identify keywords that relate to what you have to sell, and use those to try to bring people who are searching on those keywords to your products and services.

I strongly recommend that you mostly use the bottom-up approach. Starting with broadly popular keywords is likely to lead you to keywords that are only somewhat applicable to your product. At the same time, it's likely to get you into a bidding war against people with much more AdWords experience, and possibly much deeper pockets, than you.

Using the bottom-up approach, you're much more likely to identify keywords that are highly relevant to your products and services. At the same time, you're also more likely to identify the true gems: rarely used keywords that work well for you, without being helpful to other, competing advertisers.

Finding these gems is big business. There are dozens of books and online tools for keyword generation. One tool promises you "the power to slash through the fog and instantly gobble up hundreds of hot, niche-focused keywords." Another tool in the same genre is shown in Figure 11.1.

FIGURE 11.1   There are many keyword tools online.

However, you can get most of, or all, the help you need from the tools within AdWords. Start with those tools, learn them thoroughly, and check out what kind of results you get. Only then should you consider getting outside help.

> TIP: **Consider Using Geographic Targeting**
>
> Geographic targeting (see Lesson 6, "Deciding Where to Show Your Ads") can help you "win" on keywords that might be too expensive for you to consider otherwise. Just be sure to track your return on investment carefully so that you aren't winning the (keyword) battle but losing the (profitability) war.

The keyword-matching tool in AdWords is shown in Figure 11.2. To access it, within AdWords, search for "Keyword Tool" in the Help Center located on the left side of the page. Or link to it from within the Create Ad and Keywords page (also called the Create Ad page if you've already entered some keywords), as described in the steps at the end of this lesson. The Keyword Tool can generate suggested keywords by using a word or phrase as a starting point, by analyzing a website, or via both techniques together.

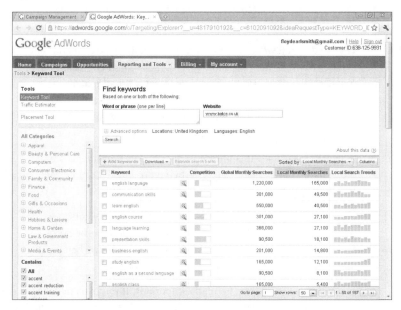

FIGURE 11.2   The AdWords Keyword matching tool is powerful.

This tool is worth experimenting with; you can return to it again and again as you gain experience with AdWords campaigns for your products and services.

TIP: **Finding the Right Keywords**

Don't worry too much that you won't find the right keywords; AdWords suggests them for you. All you have to do is come up with the best list that you can; AdWords helps you find related words until, over time, you come up with a strong list.

Using Different Types of Keywords

The way that AdWords matches keywords that you enter to the keywords users type is important to your overall success with AdWords. For instance, if you choose "red wine" as a keyword, and some users are entering "red wines," you could miss them completely.

The way that AdWords matches keywords is the same way that Google search matches keywords. However, most Google search users aren't aware of how this matching takes place. So, here are the details:

▶ **Keyword.** Somewhat oddly, entering a specific word generates matches *to all versions of that word.* Other search engines used to make you enter special characters to get a broad match, such as "win*" to get "wine," "wines," and "winery" (also "window," "winnow," and so forth). With Google search and AdWords, entering "wine" gets you "wine" and "wines," but not "winery."

▶ **"Key phrase."** Putting a phrase in quotes gets you matches only to that exact phrase. For instance, "wine products" doesn't get you "wine production."

▶ **[Keyword].** Putting a single word in square brackets gets you matches only to that exact word. You have to do this for every single variation on a word that you want to match to when creating keywords where a specific match is important.

▶ **-Keyword.** This one can be really important; it removes matches where the forbidden term appears. For instance, I sometimes do searches on the IPCC—the Intergovernmental Panel on Climate Change, which won the Nobel Peace Price in 2007 along with Al Gore. I don't want matches to the U.K.'s IPCC (the Independent Police Complaints Commission). So, when I do any kind of match to the IPCC, I include the phrase, "-police," in my search entry. That way, I get nearly all the matches to the global IPCC, and few of the matches to the U.K.'s version.

> TIP: **Using the Display Network**
>
> If you use the Display Network of websites that have signed up for AdSense, AdWords places your ads based on a combination of all your keywords, not just specific keywords, one at a time. This is probably necessary, given the challenges of matching to various blogs and so on, but means you have less control than with the Search Network. It also means that, if you're using the Display Network, you should retain some looser, broad keywords that don't work well on the Search Network to improve your Display Network matching. (Or, to increase your effectiveness, create separate campaigns for otherwise similar Search Network and Display Network advertising.)

Here are a few examples of keywords that one might consider for certain kinds of products and services:

- **Wine shop**. Start with broad terms such as [wine], [wines], "red wine," "white wine." Proceed to narrower terms such as [shiraz] and [chardonnay], and then on to brand names such as [chateau montelena].

- **Bookstore**. Broad terms include [book], [magazine], [hardcover]. Narrower terms include [fiction], [thriller], [detective] (as in "detective story"). Specific names might include [grisham] for John Grisham, [king] for Stephen King, and [bible] for the world's best-selling book.

- **Ice cream shop**. Going from broad to narrow, terms might include "ice cream," [sherbet], "chocolate ice cream," and "white chocolate chip."

Note that this is the starting list. Broad keywords are often too expensive and unproductive to be worthwhile. Not only does the keyword potentially get a lot of bidding; if your ads do display, they might not get as many clicks as, say, a nationally recognized online vendor for the same product. And if your ads get fewer clicks, AdWords gradually stops showing them.

Narrow keywords, on the other hand, are often much better. Not only do they often work well, in and of themselves, but they work in Google's Keyword Tool to help link to other, related keywords—even misspellings. (The word "chateau" alone must have a dozen near misses associated with it.)

In creating keywords for BATCS and its accent-reduction books and classes, I found that the word "elocution" was surprisingly effective, whereas the word "pronunciation" (and its various misspellings) is too heavily competed on for BATCS to be able to make much headway with it.

> TIP: **Consider Using Specific Keywords**
> Consider using specific keywords and key phrases by putting keywords in square [brackets] and key phrases in "quotation marks." That way, you only get—and only pay for—exact matches. You can gradually test many variants on a word or phrase, keeping—and paying for—only the ones that work best for you.

Keywords and Ad Text

When people are searching online, research shows, they act quickly and almost instinctively, not giving a lot of thinking time to what they see before clicking. We've all had the experience of clicking something, only to realize, a fraction of a second later, that we should have clicked something else instead.

One way to get this behavior working for you is to include keywords in your ad copy. The user is looking and clicking on the basis of recognizability; that is, the user is looking for their keyword or phrase within the text of the search results. Your AdWords ad is, in a sense, a search result. If it contains the keyword or phrase in question, it's more likely to get clicked.

Here are some examples of revisions of the BATCS accent-reduction course ads in the previous lesson to reflect various keywords. Here's the original ad:

Accent reduction course (23 characters)
Experienced teacher; London location (33 characters)

Course starts 20th October (23 characters)
www.batcs.co.uk

For the key phrase "received pronunciation," also known as RP, the headline could be rewritten thus: "Accent reduction with RP" (24 characters). It would be up to the second line, with the word "teacher," and the third line, with the word "course," to communicate that what was being offered was indeed a course.

Or the first line of description could become the following: Received pronunciation in London (32 characters). The user would know it was a course from the headline; the part about the teacher being experienced would be low.

For the keyword "elocution," the headline could be rewritten as "Elocution course" (16 characters). This loses the idea of accent reduction, so that might need to go in the first line of description: "Accent reduction; London location" (33 characters). This helps add detail to the phrase in the headline, "Elocution course," which to some might seem to refer more to manners than to pronunciation.

Elocution could also be handled in the first line only, which could become "Elocution focus; London location" (32 characters).

Entering Keywords and Key Phrases

Follow these steps to enter keywords and key phrases:

1. If you're not there already, go to AdWords and start creating a new campaign, as described in Lesson 5, "Setting Up a New Campaign." Choose the campaign type, give your campaign a name, and set the advertising networks and devices to run your ads on. Set the locations and languages, as well, as described in Lesson 6, "Deciding Where to Show Your Ads;" your bidding options and budget, as described in Lesson 7, "Setting Your Bidding, Budget, and Delivery Options;" and your extensions and advanced settings, as described in Lessons 8, "Adding Extensions," and 9, "Using Advanced Settings." Click **Continue**.

You should be on the Campaigns tab, with the Create Ad Group area displayed, as shown in Figure 10.5 in the previous lesson. (If you're using AdWords for the very first time, it shows Create Ads and keywords.)

2. Scroll down to Keywords. Enter keywords and key phrases, one per line. Use quotes around "a phrase" to get an exact match for the phrase; use square brackets around a [keyword] to get an exact match for a keyword.

If you don't use these symbols to get specific matches, you'll get a broad match instead; this might or might not be what you want.

3. To get tips on choosing effective keywords, click the **Help Me Choose Effective Keywords** link. Use the information provided to help add keywords to your list. Then close the screen and return to the previous screen, in the Campaigns tab, before continuing.

The help screen shown in Figure 11.3 appears. From within this screen, you can access the Keyword Tool by clicking the **Use the Keyword Tool** link.

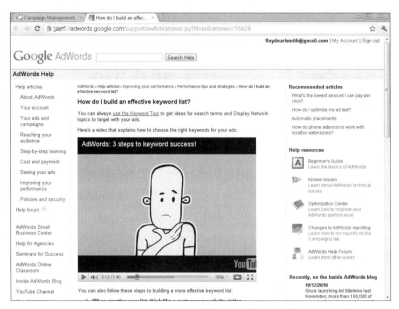

FIGURE 11.3   AdWords offers you ideas for getting your keywords right.

> **TIP: Try Keywords Singly**
>
> To get an estimate of the search traffic and cost for each keyword and key phrase, enter one phrase into the Keywords area, and then click the **Estimate Search Traffic** button. You'll get a specific estimate. Consider saving the overall list of keywords in a word processing program, and copying the search traffic and cost estimates into a spreadsheet for comparison.

4. To get an estimate of search traffic, and the resulting cost per click, click the **Estimate Search Traffic** button.

   An estimate of search traffic appears, as shown in Figure 11.4. Note that the estimates are approximate, but they do give you a comparative idea of how different keywords and groups of keywords might perform, as well as how much they might cost.

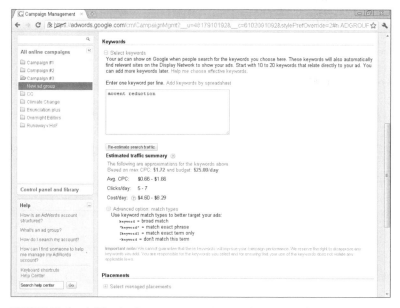

FIGURE 11.4   AdWords gives you an estimate of search traffic.

5. To save your work so far, click the **Save Ad Group button**.

   Then, to complete work on the ad group, go to the next lesson.

Summary

In this lesson, you learned how to generate keywords from the bottom up, based on the products and services you sell, as well as how to adjust your ads to reflect keywords. You were then shown keyword tools and techniques for specifying different types of keywords, as well as how to enter keywords and key phrases for your campaign, generating cost and search traffic estimates along the way.

LESSON 12

Choosing Placements and Bids

In this lesson, you learn how to choose placements for Display Network ads and whether to specify sites to include or to exclude from Display Network advertising. You also learn how to set maximum cost-per-click (CPC) amounts for Search Network ads, Display Network ads, and managed placements, and how to save your ad group settings.

Choosing Placements

Placements are a tool you can use for managing how your ads appear in the Display Network, which consists of websites that use Google AdSense to place Google ads from advertisers like yourself on their sites.

> TIP: **Mastering Search Advertising**
> Search advertising, as described throughout this book, builds your AdWords skills. Consider gaining some mastery of search advertising before taking on Display Network advertising.

Most AdWords advertisers begin with text ads shown on the Search Network, as recommended in this book. However, after you get experience with text ads—or, right from the beginning, if you have specific needs— you might want to consider using the Display Network and managed placements. Google is increasing its support for the Display Network with many new tools, as shown in Figure 12.1.

FIGURE 12.1   The Display Network is getting more love from Google.

> TIP: **Getting Over the Hump**
>
> The main challenge of using the Display Network is the research you need to undertake to see what specific sites might work for you and which ones to exclude. After you start doing this work, using the Display Network, and managed placements in particular, can make a lot of sense.

The problem with the Display Network is that it's a bit of a mixed bag—a mix of mostly medium-sized sites that can vary widely in how useful they are for your particular ad. For instance, to reuse an earlier example, let's suppose you want to sell footballs. Sites that have the word "football" might be for people who want to play—or who only want to watch. Depending on whether you're selling footballs to toss around with the kids, or signed memorabilia desired by sports fans, different sites with the word "football" in them might or might not be very helpful to you.

Managed placements can help—if you're willing to bite the bullet—and enable you to do a couple of interesting things:

▶ **Adding placements.** You can run ads only on specific sites that you choose. Use the campaign setting to run ads on the Display Network, as described in Lesson 3, "Creating Your First AdWords Campaign," but only on Relevant Pages Only on the Placements I Manage. Then use the Placements area, described here, to specify which sites to use.

▶ **Removing placements.** If you're running ads across the Display Network, you can remove placements you dislike—again, using the Placements area.

▶ **Bid management.** You can run ads across the Display Network, but use higher or lower bids on specific sites that meet your needs better or less well than others. How to do this is described in the next section of this lesson.

By contrast, most ads on the Display Network are placed automatically, rather than by managed placement. Automatic placements are determined by matches between a site and your entire list of keywords.

Follow these steps to set up managed placements:

1. If you're not there already, go to AdWords and go through most of the steps to create a new campaign, as described in Lessons 5, "Setting Up a New Campaign," through 11, "Finding Your Keywords."

   You should be on the Campaigns tab, with the Create Ad Group area displayed at the top of the page, as shown in Figure 10.5.

2. Scroll down to the Placements area. Click the **Select Managed Placements** link to open up the options for managed placements.

   You'll see two areas: one for entering specific placements, another for getting placement ideas.

3. To enter specific placements, enter the name of the site or area of the site.

The name of a site is simply the home page URL, such as
www.pearson.com for the entire Pearson publishing website. To
advertise in a specific directory of the website, enter the URL for
that area of the site, such as www.pearson.com/media-1 for the
Media area.

TIP: **Manage Research Time Carefully**

It can be a lot of fun to find sites, and areas of sites, that are
friendly to your ads, but it's worth it only if the site gets a lot of
traffic, and if you're going to be bidding enough to get your ad
shown on the site. Manage your time carefully as you begin using
managed placements so that you get a good return on the investment of your time and effort.

4. To exclude specific placements, enter the name of the site or area
   of the site, preceded by a minus sign.

   The site, or area of a site, will be excluded.

5. To get tips on potentially valuable placements (or not valuable
   ones), enter a word, phrase, or website name in the text box
   under Get Placement Ideas. Then click **Search**.

   You'll see websites, ad formats supported, and impressions per
   day in the results, as shown in Figure 12.2. You can enter words,
   phrases, and websites to help identify sites to exclude and sites to
   include.

6. Use the suggestions from the placement ideas search to include
   or exclude specific sites, as described in steps 3 and 4.

7. If you have allowed AdWords to manage your maximum cost per
   click, as described in Lesson 7, "Setting Your Bidding, Budget,
   and Delivery Options," this is the last step in setting up your ad
   group. Click the **Save Ad Group** button.

   The ad group is saved, and you see the reporting screen for your
   ad group, as described in the next section.

FIGURE 12.2   Google will help you find placements for your ads.

Entering Default Bids

Setting bids for keywords is one of the most interesting, exciting—and potentially expensive—decisions you can make in using AdWords. The maximum CPC that you set here is just one of several ways to influence the actual cost you pay per click.

> **NOTE: Cost Per Click (CPC) and Ad Displays**
>
> Setting a high CPC bid won't necessarily get your ad displayed. The ad has to attract clicks when it is shown; otherwise, AdWords will quickly rate its attractiveness low and stop showing it. So, you need both a solid CPC bid and attractive creative to get your ads shown.

If you made specific choices for your settings, as described next, you get the option of setting default bids for your ads, as shown in Figure 12.3.

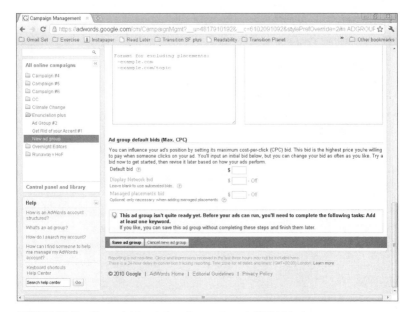

FIGURE 12.3   You might get the chance to set CPC bids here.

Here are factors that affect your actual cost per click for search network ads:

- ▶ **Automatic Bidding.** If you set this option, you can let AdWords set the budget for you. You don't need to set a maximum CPC, although you're given the option. See Lesson 7 for details. You don't see the option to enter default bids on this screen.

- ▶ **Group Default Bid.** This setting, described here, is a default maximum CPC for the group as a whole. You can enter different (higher or lower) bids for specific keywords, overriding the group default bid for that keyword.

- ▶ **Specific Keyword Bids.** Bids you enter for specific keywords override the group default bid you enter here.

The rationale for entering various bids for your overall campaign, and for different keywords, depends entirely on your business proposition. To reuse our earlier example, if you're selling footballs signed by Brett Favre, the keyword "football" will be worth something to you, "signed football" will be worth more, and "Brett Favre signed football" (or some other strong variation) even more than that.

But if you're selling unsigned footballs, the latter phrases won't be valuable at all. You have to make your best guess on the value of clicks in a campaign, and of specific keywords, and then adjust as your advertising results indicate.

You can also enter bids that affect ads on the Display Network:

▶ **Display Network bid.** You can enter a CPC bid for clicks from the Display Network. A higher bid is likely to get your ad displayed more. If you leave this field blank, the word "Auto" will appear, and the amount used by AdWords will derive from your other CPC bids.

▶ **Managed Placements bid.** You can enter a separate CPC for managed placements. If you don't, the Display Network bid is used, if you enter one.

The rationale for entering a higher or lower bid for ads on the Display Network, and for managed placements, also varies depending on your business. Because Display Network ads are targeted to sites based on all your keywords together, the value of these ads is generally believed to be near the low end of what you're willing to pay per click on the Search Network. Part of the rationale for using managed placements is to overcome this imprecision and raise the value of your Display Network advertising.

Follow these steps to enter default CPC bids for your ad group:

1. If you're not there already, go to AdWords and go through most of the steps to create a new campaign, as described in Lessons 5 through 11.

   You should be on the Campaigns tab, with the Create Ad and Keywords area displayed at the top of the page, as shown in Figure 10.5. (If you've previously defined keywords, it will be called the Create Ad Group area.)

2. Scroll down to the Ad Group Default Bids (Max. CPC) area.

   This area appears only if you have not allowed AdWords to manage bids for you, as described previously in this section. It's shown in Figure 12.3.

3. To specify a default bid for the ad group, enter an amount next to the Default Bid prompt. You must enter a bid here.

   This bid is used for all keywords for which you don't enter a specific bid.

4. To specify a bid for Display Network ads, enter an amount next to the Display Network Bid prompt. You're not required to enter a bid here.

   This bid is used for all Display Network ads except managed placements, if you use them and enter a separate bid for them, as described in the next step.

5. To specify a bid for managed placements, enter an amount next to the Managed Placements Bid prompt. You're not required to enter a bid here.

   This bid is used for managed placements only.

6. Click the **Save Ad Group** button.

   The ad group is saved, and you see the reporting screen for your ad group, as described in the next lesson.

Summary

In this lesson, you learned how to choose placements for Display Network ads, whether to specify sites to include or to exclude from Display Network advertising. You also learned how to set maximum CPC amounts for search network ads, Display Network ads, and managed placements, and how to save your ad group settings.

LESSON 13

Managing Your Ad Group

In this lesson, you learn how to understand the wide variety of keyword-related information that AdWords displays for an ad group. You also learn how to analyze the success of different keywords and how to improve your campaign for better performance.

Understanding the Ad Group Screen

You can have several ad groups in a campaign. An ad group can have a single ad, a pair of ads being tested against each other, or a set of more or less related ads. For instance, you can have several similar ads, with slight variations to include the particular keywords that the ad runs with. That way, you can use well-tested text while adhering to the suggestion that ads contain the keyword that the user typed.

In this lesson, I show you the high points of the ad group screen, which has a great deal going on. I start with a new group that has just been created and not yet had any ads shown because that's where you'll be started.

I then show highlights of the ad group screen for a campaign that's been running for a week. This brings to life the various reporting aspects and controls in the ad group screen. Finally, I show some of the key settings you can change to improve your campaign.

The Ad Group screen is shown in Figure 13.1. In the figure, the ad group has no data. This is how the screen looks when you create a new ad group.

The ad and key settings   Time period for reporting

Details - Column headings   Graphs

FIGURE 13.1   The Ad Group screen says a lot even with no data.

Even a few hours after your ads start running, you won't see any data on the Ad Group screen. It almost always takes AdWords several hours to reflect any changes you make, monitor the results, and report back. Although this is totally understandable, it's one of the most frustrating aspects of using AdWords.

In its search operations and other efforts, Google demonstrates a deep understanding of the importance of fast response times. Google engineers spend endless hours shaving fractions of a second off of search response times. But with AdWords, you can have a great idea, try it—and then have to wait several hours before receiving even the most initial feedback.

As a result, using AdWords effectively takes focus and dedication. When you try something new, you have to keep checking back, and make decisions as quickly as possible whether to stick with a change, revert to previous settings, or try something else new.

Figure 13.1 shows the Ad Group screen for a new ad group, with no data received yet. Highlights include the following:

▶ **The ad and key settings.** The ads are shown in the upper left, along with key settings—how cost-per-click (CPC) is managed for the ad group, the default bid, if any, and more.

▶ **Time period for reporting.** AdWords reporting is flexible, but you need to keep checking different reporting periods to get a useful picture of what's going on. You also need to track information such as changes you make for the charts and graphs to be truly useful. (AdWords does have a View Change History link to help, but you should still keep your own records.)

▶ **Graphs.** Although the graph area doesn't show anything at first, as it fills in, it's one of the most important tools for efficiently keeping on top of your ad campaign.

▶ **Clicks and Impressions.** Most AdWords advertisers want clicks because these lead directly to purchases or other desirable actions. Impressions are good to know, both because they have some inherent value and because they help you understand the click-through rate of a keyword—a critical statistic.

▶ **CTR.** The click-through rate tells you how powerful your ads are. A high click-through rate not only brings you customers, AdWords takes it into account as a reason to keep showing your ad, even if your keyword bids are lower than competitors'. A compelling offer, and a good underlying value proposition, will keep users clicking.

▶ **Avg. CPC.** The average cost per click is important, but it's only one part of the equation for you as an advertiser. You need to find ways to understand how clicks on a given keyword translate into sales to advertise whether a given CPC is a bargain or a minor economic tragedy.

▶ **Cost.** Cost is important, but only in proportion to benefit—ultimately, the profits you make from sales that begin with your ad.

▶ **Average Position.** AdWords places a premium on top positions for your ad. The top one or two ads might appear above organic search results, and on mobile phones, results beyond the first one or two are sharply less likely to be seen. But some campaigns do well by moderating spending and having ads show up in lesser positions. Managing cost versus average position for different ads, offers, and products and services is part of the art of using AdWords.

> NOTE: **Why CTR Matters**
>
> A high click-through rate (CTR) on a keyword indicates that the keyword and your ad are really working well together. First, check whether the keyword and ad are really likely to drive sales for you. Then look for similar keywords and check whether you can improve your ad further. Also see whether there's the opportunity to create additional ads that will help other keywords get a high CTR, too.

Monitoring and Changing Your Account

There are two schools of thought about making changes to your account. One is to tweak it frequently, constantly working to improve it for best results. The idea here is that you're spending money on AdWords every day, so why not get the most out of it every day? The other approach is to set things up, and then let them run for a while. This gives you stability and reasonably long periods to monitor your results and make sure they're meaningful. That way, when you do make changes, they're more likely to be good ones. The idea behind this approach is that AdWords is a long-term investment, so why not treat it like one?

There are good reasons for waiting various lengths of time:

> ▶ **A day.** It's probably a good idea to let changes sit for at least a day before making more changes. It takes changes a few hours to show up in your reporting anyway, and people's Internet behavior is drastically different during different parts of the day. So, you probably want to wait at least a day between changes.

▶ **A week.** Just as people's Internet behavior changes over the course of a day, it's certainly different over a period of a week—in particular, weekdays versus weekend days. Waiting a week gives you a sense of what might work in one period versus the other.

▶ **A month.** Months are funny because they have significantly different numbers of days, and because the "extra" days—the days additional to the 28-day, 4-week core that all months have—can have a different impact depending on how many of them are weekdays versus weekend days. Many seeming trends within a month, and between one month and another, are just artifacts of different numbers of days, and of weekdays versus weekend days. However, month-to-month comparisons are valuable. You have to adjust them for the number of days in the month, though—and if you get much different results on weekends and weekdays, for that factor, as well.

▶ **A quarter.** Whereas months can vary a lot, things smooth out much more over a calendar quarter. Calendar quarters also map fairly closely to seasons, so you can take seasonal variations, and the holiday-heavy fourth calendar quarter, into account when analyzing your results.

TIP: **Quarters Are More Comparable Than Years**

Quarters are only slightly different in length: 90 days for Q1 (or 91 in leap year), 91 days for Q2, and 92 days each for Q3 and Q4. The percentage difference is much less than for months. Months all have at least 28 days, but can have 0 to 3 more days, more than a 10% variation. Additionally, from 0 to 3 of the "extra" days can be weekends or holidays, making comparability more difficult. For quarters, the base is 91 days—13 weeks—and the variation is only 1 day fewer or more, a variation of just over 1%.

▶ **Years.** It might seem a distant prospect now, when you're just starting out with AdWords, but year-to-year comparisons smooth out just about all variations and give you a solid background for comparison. Of course, the technological base and the competitive landscape are likely to change over that time as Google changes its search and AdWords offerings and the economy improves or declines, but that's always the case.

> NOTE: **School's out for Summer**
>
> A wildcard in understanding your AdWords performance over time is school schedules. If your product or service has many customers 21 or under, you are likely to be heavily affected by the various school terms that students are on. You either need to track the schedules of your particular customer base very closely, or use quarterly measurements—with Q3 being almost all holiday, Q4 being almost half holiday, and Q1 and Q2 being almost solid in-school periods for most students.

Figure 13.2 shows results over one week—from Wednesday through Tuesday—for a campaign. (The next lesson shows you how to get reports on different criteria, and covering different time periods.) Note the sharp dip on Friday, and the strong results for Sunday, Monday, and Tuesday.

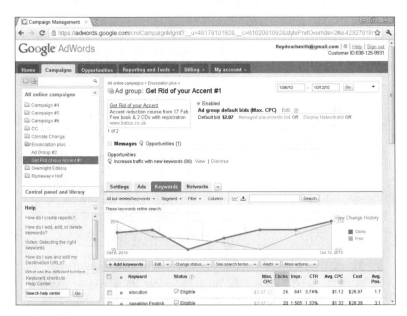

FIGURE 13.2   Some ad groups do much better on weekdays.

Both approaches—making changes opportunistically versus less often—have their good points. When you're first starting out, though, you might want to consider a hybrid strategy.

Make a lot of changes for the first day or two. Don't take your early, partial results as if they were definitive, but do use them to generate ideas. Throw a lot of stuff at the wall.

What kinds of changes might you make in the early days? Here's a "top 10" list of the main changes to consider:

1. **Additional one-word keywords**. See which keywords are working for you—which ones generate a lot of clicks, and which ones have a high click-through rate. Look for variations on, and synonyms of, those words. In helping BATCS with its accent reduction offerings, a keyword that the proprietor knew would work, but I didn't— "elocution"—has been the strongest for generating clicks and for CTR, as well.

2. **Additional keyword phrases**. Think of single-word keywords as the branches of your AdWords tree, and phrases that include those keywords as leaves coming off the branches. Experiment aggressively with keyword phrases. Use phrases with one specific keyword to give you ideas for phrases including different keywords.

3. **Keyword bids**. Try to understand which keywords map most closely to making sales and profits, and consider increasing your keyword bids on those to help drive more sales and more profits.

4. **Overall budget**. Try to understand how profitable your AdWords effort is, based on feedback about how much it's improving your profitability. Make changes in your budget to reflect this. Don't run at a loss (or an unknown impact) for long, though; if you can't make a profit fairly quickly, consider cutting your losses.

5. **Additional ads and offers**. Try out different "creative" on your customer base. Experiment with different offers. Try really dramatic offers, such as half-price offers, to see what kind of response you get. (Pull the ad quickly if it's costing you too much money!)

6. **Additional products and services**. Consider specific ads for specific products and services.

7. **Custom ads**. Consider creating a custom ad for each of your stronger keywords. The custom ad should include the specific keyword, which tends to improve click-through rate. Combine this with your other experiments with ads and ad text.

8. **Landing pages**. Consider creating more landing pages, more closely tailored to different ads or groups of ads, as explained in Lesson 15, "Using Opportunities and Improving Landing Pages."

9. **The Display Network**. Consider using what you've learned to advertise on the Display Network. Create a separate campaign, and use a subset of your keywords (the best ones that, together, tell a story) and your best creative. Then vary it for the somewhat different Display Network audience.

10. **Display ads**. After you've improved your keyword choices and changed your text ads to improve your click-through rate, consider creating different kinds of ads that reflect what you've learned.

Make changes (as described in the next lesson) based on the preceding list. Then wait awhile and see what sticks. It's a good idea to review your AdWords account on a regular basis and see what's working or not. Ask customers whether they used AdWords to find you—and, if so, what they thought of the process.

After the initial period, when you're making changes and checking them daily, I recommend that you review your AdWords progress weekly—that is, every single week. Write down what changes you make, and why; if you don't make any, note that, too. See what's working and what's not. Consider changes based on whether you're coming into a holiday period, the weather, school being in or out of session, whether you're planning a sale, and any other real-world variations that affect your business.

Work to gradually improve your ability to understand where AdWords is and isn't working for you. First, find a way to ensure that you know whether your AdWords investment as a whole is paying off—not just in increased revenue, but in increased profit. Then figure out how to get at least a rough idea of the value of specific ads and keywords. This will be the basis for gradual improvements to your AdWords presence.

Analyzing Keyword Success

Your AdWords spending, and your AdWords success, is all down to key-words. Impressions are nice, but they don't cost you anything directly. It's the combination of keywords, ad copy, clicks, and your landing page that drive business directly to you. Keywords are crucial to this.

Figure 13.3 shows keyword results for the Get Rid of Your Accent ad group. The results are sorted by the number of clicks each keyword generates.

> TIP: **Keeping Track of Changes**
>
> Consider keeping a written record of all changes you make in each of your AdWords ad groups. Include your reasons for making changes. Note what ad text you were using, what the results were—clicks, impressions, CTR, spending, and so on. Record the results during the period when each setup was in place. Having this information handy will help you avoid mistakes and converge on a steadily improving approach to your AdWords advertising.

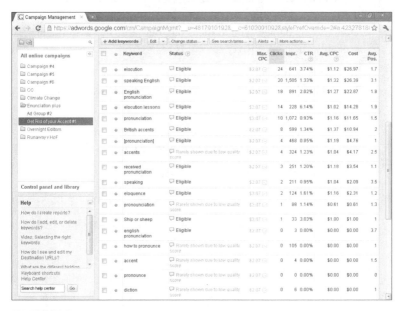

FIGURE 13.3   Keyword success is the secret of AdWords.

By clicking at the top of a column, you can sort by any of the categories. Follow these steps:

1. Go to the Campaigns tab and select the specific ad group you want to analyze. Click the name to bring it onscreen. Scroll down to see your keywords and the categories they're displayed in.

   The column header remains in place even if you scroll down through a very long list of keywords.

2. Click the **Keyword** column header to sort the column by keyword in alphabetic order. Click again to sort it in reverse alphabetic order.

3. Click any column header to sort the data by the values in that column. Click again to sort it in reverse order.

   The column sorts in order by the value in the column whose header you clicked.

   I recommend that you use a sort by the number of clicks, in descending order—the keyword with the most clicks shows up in the first row—as your most common view on your keywords. Doing so encourages you to focus on your most successful (and, probably, most expensive) keywords first.

4. To see the information in a spreadsheet view, as shown in Figure 13.4, choose select **Spreadsheet Edit** from the More Actions pull-down.

   The view changes. You can make changes, within reason, and they are reflected in the workings of your ad group.

5. To return to the previous view, click **Cancel**.

   The view changes back to the table view shown in Figure 13.3.

6. To compare one number, such as clicks, to another, such as costs, use the reporting features described in the next lesson.

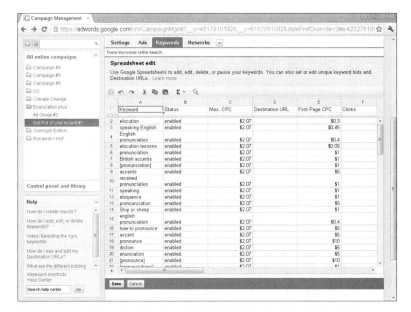

FIGURE 13.4 You can edit your campaign in Google Spreadsheets.

You can use each and every category to help improve your ad group and your overall AdWords campaign. Here are some tips on getting the most out of this information:

> ▶ **Keyword.** Use keywords that show up at the top of various sort-ings—number of clicks and click-through rate being crucial—to generate related keywords, such as variations, synonyms, and even misspellings, and keyword-based phrases.

CAUTION: **Instant Search**

Google's Instant Search feature, introduced late in 2010, encour-ages users to click away from their searches after typing just a sin-gle word, or even part of a word. Concentrate first on one-word key-words to improve your results, and only then on keyword-based phrases.

▶ **Status.** When you see the words "Rarely shown due to low Quality Score," that means that your max CPC low click-through rate is not high enough to beat competitors for the AdWords showings you want. If the keyword in question is valuable to you, consider raising your CPC and improving your creative to see whether your results improve.

▶ **Max. CPC.** If the word "Auto" appears here, that indicates that you're letting Google set the amount. The max CPC is a problem only if your average CPC, and therefore the total cost, is too high. (Occasionally paying $2 a click doesn't really hurt you if the average is closer to $1 a click.)

TIP: **Changing the Maximum CPC**

If you've set up your campaign to let AdWords manage the maximum CPC for you, you have to change it there; see Lesson 7, "Setting Your Bidding, Budget, and Delivery Options." If you've set your campaign so that you manage the maximum CPC yourself, click **Max. CPC for a Keyword** to make adjustments.

▶ **Clicks.** This is what you're fighting for with your keyword choices and ad copy! It's through clicks that you get people to your landing page and doing business with you. Think in terms of maximizing your clicks per day and controlling your daily budget—these are the key factors.

▶ **Impressions.** Impressions do have some value, but it's hard to know how much. If you do other advertising, such as in a local newspaper or Yellow Pages directory, you can compare the cost per impression for AdWords to the other media to see which is the better deal, on an impressions basis. (AdWords has the additional advantage of driving clicks, of course.)

▶ **CTR (Click-Through Rate).** A high CTR and a high number of impressions can somewhat offset each other—having either high can generate a large number of clicks overall. What a high CTR is particularly good for is identifying hot keywords that draw users to you. Any CTR over 2% can be considered quite good for most purposes. Note that several of the keywords in the figure have a CTR higher than 2%, including "elocution," at nearly 4%, and "elocution lessons," at a very high rate of more than 6%.

> TIP: **Keywords Versus Key Phrases**
>
> It's common for hot keywords to serve as the base of even hotter keyword phrases. Although it's hard work to find the right phrases, and though impressions for the phrase are bound to be lower than impressions for the keyword by itself, the high CTR of the best keyword phrases can make all the effort worthwhile.

▶ **Avg. CPC.** Your average CPC for all your keywords, times your total clicks, determines your total cost. Your average CPC for your most-clicked keywords has the biggest impact, so manage this carefully.

▶ **Cost.** Your cost per keyword or keyword phrase is determined by the clicks you get times the average cost per click. Compare the cost of your most popular keywords to the total daily cost, and focus efforts such as improving your ads on the "big spenders" to get the most out of your overall campaign.

▶ **Avg. Pos.** The average display position of your ad is something you can manage. If you have compelling ads and good success in getting the ads shown, lowering your maximum CPC can lower your cost and your average display position—without necessarily reducing your clicks very much. Experiment with this to see whether you can get very similar results with a sharply lower outlay.

There is a lot of power in the ability that AdWords provides to view your keywords' relative success in an interactive table. However, you might want to use some things for analysis that that aren't available through the table. For instance, I prefer to see percentages rather than raw numbers. For all its many capabilities, the AdWords keyword display doesn't show percentages.

If you want to do further processing on the information, set the date range that you want, and then download the information as a report. (How to do so is described in detail in the next lesson.) You can then analyze the information to your heart's content.

There are also things that a report like this can't tell you. For instance, the ad that drives the most clicks might not actually drive the most sales. Try to think like a customer who's searching on a specific word or phrase and sees your ad. What would drive that customer to click it? Can you reword the ad to make sure that the people who click are people who are likely to buy?

Summary

In this lesson, you learned how to understand the wide variety of keyword-related information that AdWords displays for an ad group. You also learned how to analyze the success of different keywords and how to improve your campaign for better performance.

Updating Your Campaign

In this lesson, you learn how to create and understand reports, including setting date ranges and choosing from among the many available options. You also learn how to add new ads to your campaign and how to create alerts to help monitor performance.

Creating and Understanding Reports

The best feature of AdWords might be its reporting capabilities. You get a great deal of feedback from AdWords and much of what you see is interactive—you can change the report, and sometimes even the underlying settings, just by clicking what you're seeing onscreen.

The keyword performance display described in Lesson 13, "Managing Your Ad Group," is, in effect, a report. The columns are all sortable, it's easily opened in a live spreadsheet (or exported to a not-live one), and the reporting period can be easily changed, as described in this lesson.

> **TIP: Setting Alerts**
> You can set an *alert*—a request to be updated when your account matches or exceeds certain criteria—under either the Keywords or Ads tab. Setting alerts is described in the next section, "Managing Ads and Alerts."

AdWords also has interactive reporting built in to the Campaigns tab and also in a separate Reporting and Tools tab. In addition, Google offers Google Analytics, a sophisticated, but still free tool that offers powerful capabilities for managing your website, including the source of visits to the site. As an AdWords user, AdWords should be the origin of many such visits.

The reports in the Campaigns tab are enough for most businesses to get started. In this section, I focus on helping you get the most out of them, and show you how to change settings and create new ads, which might visibly improve your results.

I concentrate on reports at the ad group level. You can also get similar reports at the campaign level, which combines statistics from all the ad groups in one campaign into one report. The workings are the same, but the totals are simply comprehensive rather than ad group specific. Also, at the campaign level, you can't see individual keywords and their results; you have to go into ad groups for that.

Setting the Date Range for Reporting

Within the Campaigns tab, to view keyword performance, you will often select an ad group and choose the Keywords subtab. Underneath the Keywords subtab, a report shows campaign performance for one or more variables over a specified period of time. The keywords list beneath the report also includes statistics for the same period of time.

To set the time period for reports, including the keywords list and associated statistics, use the Date Range pull-down, as shown in Figure 14.1. You have a range of choices for the date range:

▶ **Custom Date Range.** You enter the start and end dates.

▶ **Today or Yesterday.** When selecting any time period that includes the current day—or the previous day, if it's early in the morning—remember that statistics in AdWords are always a few hours behind actual events.

▶ **This Week (beginning either Sunday or Monday).** You can get the current week with either starting day you choose.

▶ **Last 7 Days.** This is a useful selection because it takes into account a representative number of weekdays and weekend days.

▶ **Last Week (beginning either Sunday or Monday, or the last business week, Monday through Friday).** This is the previous week—a full week, with either starting day you choose, or just the business week.

▶ **Last 14 Days.** As with the Last 7 days option, this is a useful selection because it includes a representative number of weekdays and weekends.

▶ **This Month; Last 30 Days; Last Month.** These time periods are all month related, and are likely to include an unbalanced number of weekdays and weekend days.

▶ **All time.** This is simply all the data for the entire period in which you've had the account.

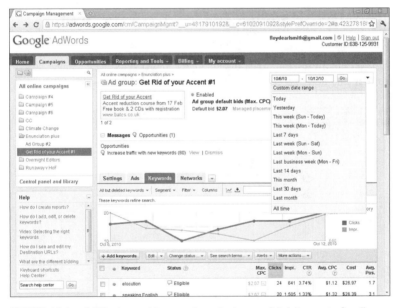

FIGURE 14.1   AdWords enables you to select a useful date range for display and reporting.

Use the date range selections to create displays that are valuable to you and show how your AdWords campaign is performing. Be sure to make note of changes that you make and events, such as changes to your ads, special promotions, or holidays, that affect your AdWords results.

Even though all these time periods are valuable for a quick inspection, they're most useful for creating reports that then go into a spreadsheet for further analysis. Using a spreadsheet enables you to do month-to-month comparisons, with adjustments for variables that are important to you, such as weekend days and holidays.

> TIP: **Manage Your Account Regularly**
> Use reporting capabilities of AdWords to help you review and update your account regularly. This might include loading data into a spreadsheet for further review and analysis.

Specifying Keywords, Segments, and Filters

Several tiny little drop-down menus under the Keywords tab enable you to further fine-tune reports, as shown in Figure 14.2. These are as follows:

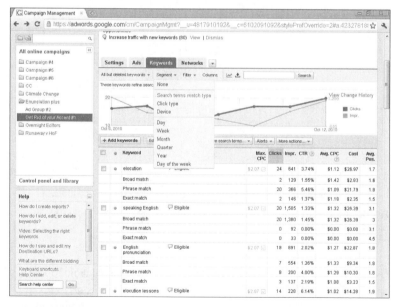

FIGURE 14.2   You can carefully fine-tune displayed information.

▶ **Keywords.** You can choose to report on all keywords, or all but deleted keywords—removing keywords you've expunged from the display and reports.

▶ **Segment.** You can break results down to show none, or no segmentation; the search terms match type (whether a match is broad, a phrase match, or an exact match), as shown in Figure 14.2; the click type, if you've activated extensions to enable additional types of clicks (such as product clicks), as described in Lesson 8, "Adding Extensions;" the device—computers versus mobile devices, for instance, as described in Lesson 9, "Using Advanced Settings;" and breakdowns by day, week, month, quarter, year, or day of the week.

▶ **Filter.** You can filter the results to show only those where the click-through rate, for instance, is above or below a certain percentage. Variables you can filter for are Cost; Avg. CPC; Avg. CPM (Cost Per thousand iMpressions); CTR; Avg. Position; Clicks; Impressions; Keyword text containing, not containing, or starting with specific characters, words or phrases; Match type for the keyword (Exact, Phrase, or Broad); Default Max. CPC above or below a value; Status (Eligible, etc.); Destination URL containing, not containing, or starting with specific characters, words or phrases; and Quality Score above or below a certain value.

▶ **Columns.** You can specify columns for the display, including specific attributes or performance metrics. You can reorder the display, too, as shown in Figure 14.3.

▶ **Downloading reports.** To download a report at any point, click the **Download Report** button (downward-pointing arrow). You can change the report name; choose a format (Excel .csv, .csv, .tsv, .xml, .pdf, .csv.gz, or .xml.gz); and add multiple segmentations by the same criteria listed in the Segment bullet earlier. You can also email the report to specific people, based on their account access to the AdWords account.

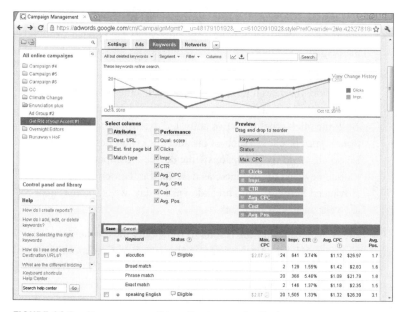

FIGURE 14.3   You can reconfigure the keywords display.

▶ **Search.** You can search the currently displayed keywords information at any point. Just enter a search term and click the
Search button. Relevant lines in the report, and ad group totals,
are displayed.

Specifying Graph Options

The most exciting and visible feature of the Keywords tab of the Ad
Group screen is the chart. However, it isn't immediately obvious how to
update the chart to show what you want. Follow these steps:

1. Click the **Toggle Graph Options** icon.

Graph options display, as shown in Figure 14.4.

2. To turn the graph display on or off, click the **Show Graph** check
box to set it or clear it.

The graph will display or be hidden to reflect the setting you
choose.

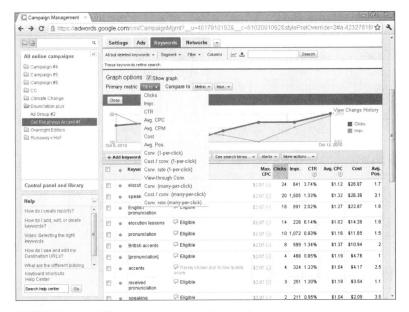

FIGURE 14.4   AdWords gives you reporting options.

3. Choose the primary metric from among similar options as the filter option in the previous section: Clicks, Impressions, CTR, Avg. CPC, Avg. CPM, Cost, Avg. Pos., and choices that include one-per-click or many-per-click options: Conv., Cost / conv., and Conv. Rate; plus View-through Conv.

   The graph updates to reflect the primary metric you choose.

4. Optionally, enter a comparison metric. You can compare to the same metric, but over a different date range, or to the same options as the primary metric.

   Using a secondary metric gives valuable context to your choice. One valuable comparison is Clicks to Metrics, although they do tend to rise and fall together.

   The graph updates to reflect the secondary metric you choose.

> NOTE: **Changing Settings**
>
> You can change settings for your campaign by choosing the **Settings** tab and then clicking the **Change Campaign Settings** link. You are given the opportunity to change the settings for the campaign, as described in Lessons 3, "Creating Your First AdWords Campaign," through 12, "Choosing Placements and Bids." The changes affect all the ad groups in the campaign. To change the settings without affecting all ad groups, create a new campaign, as described in Lesson 2, "Creating an AdWords Account," and create ad groups that fit the settings for the new campaign. You can also change the networks for a specific ad group by choosing the **Network** tab and turning on or off options such as the **Google Search Network**, the **Search Partners Network, Managed Placements**, and **Automatic Placements**.

Managing Ads and Alerts

You can create new ads for an ad group, similar to the process of creating an ad described in Lesson 10, "Writing Great Ads." Just click the **Ads** tab and choose a type of ad from the New Ad pull-down. As in creating an ad for a new campaign, choices include the following:

▶ Text ad

▶ Image ad

▶ Display ad builder

▶ Video or audio ad

▶ WAP mobile ad

You can also create an alert, which can be valuable for managing your account. Alerts appear in the message section for your account; you can also get an alert by email.

Follow these steps to create an alert:

1. Click the **Alerts** pull-down menu. Choose **Create a Custom Alert**.

The Create a Custom Alert area appears, as shown in Figure 14.5.

2. Choose the alert type: Cost, Avg. CPC, CTR, Avg. Position, Number of Clicks, or Number of Impressions.

These choices can help you keep the cost of your effort from rising to too high a level, or keep the effectiveness from falling below minimums that you determine.

3. Choose the comparison you want: Greater Than or Less Than a certain amount.

For the number of clicks, you can specify the percentage of change, as compared to selected ads or all ads in the group.

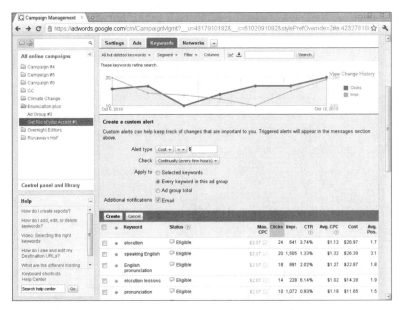

FIGURE 14.5   Set alerts to keep on top of your AdWords effort.

4. Specify whether to get a notification by email; click to set or clear the check box.

5. Specify how often to check – daily, or continually (every few hours).

6. Select whether to apply the alert to selected keywords, every keyword in the ad group, or the ad group as a whole.

7. Click **Create** to create the alert.

The alert is created. To manage alerts, choose **Manage Custom Alerts** from the pull-down menu.

Summary

In this lesson, you learned how to create and understand reports, including setting date ranges and choosing from among the many available options. You also learned how to add new ads to your campaign and how to create alerts to help monitor performance.

LESSON 15

Using Opportunities and Improving Landing Pages

In this lesson, you learn how to use the Opportunities feature in AdWords to improve your keywords and get more clicks for your ads. You also learn how to improve the landing pages on your site to improve your conversion rate from clicks to actual sales.

Taking Advantage of AdWords' Opportunities

The Opportunities feature of AdWords gets its own tab in AdWords, which is precious onscreen real estate indeed. It may well be worthwhile, too: AdWords is your opportunity to get Google's best (automated) advice on your AdWords campaign. It's worth taking advantage of.

Briefly, the tool that AdWords makes available in the Opportunities tab offers suggestions for keywords that might generate clicks for your AdWords ads. You will probably want to add at least some of the keywords to your campaign. Then let them run for a while, comparing them to your existing keywords. You can then keep the stronger keywords and remove the weaker ones, whether they're older or newer.

When should you not add a keyword suggested within the Opportunities tab? Consider these possible "knockout" considerations for a given keyword:

▶ **Wrong meaning.** In the later example for BATCS, some of the keywords suggested are for "British accent" and similar phrases, which fit the U.K. and British English focus of BATCS; others include the words "American" or "Australian." These keywords might get some clicks for BATCS, but the clicks, and the money spent on them, will be wasted. The potential customers will have to figure out from the BATCS website that they won't actually get help with achieving anything other than a British accent from BATCS.

▶ **Wrong number of searches.** A low number of searches against a given term might indicate a golden keyword that will return a lot of hits, as a percentage—or one that won't be worth your time to hassle with. You'll get a feel for this factor as you work with AdWords. However, a good click-through rate is 5%; at that click-through rate, and perfect success in getting your ad shown, 1,000 monthly searches will generate 50 clicks. If you're geo-targeting, the result might be much less. (If your geo-targeting is for New York City, for instance, and the keyword is "New York Yankees," you might still keep most of those clicks.)

▶ **Wrong level of competition.** If competition for a keyword is high, that probably means it will be expensive to get ads based on that keyword to display. Unless the meaning of the keyword is a good fit for your target audience and product or service, it might not be worth the effort to try to beat the competition around the given keyword. (A clever ad that gets lots of clicks, without resorting to tricks, might make the difference though.)

In general, you want to prioritize keywords that have a meaning that's a great fit for your product or service, that have a high number of searches, and that have less competition. You can also compare AdWords' suggestions to the keywords you already use to see which are more likely to be winners.

Consider cherry-picking the top 10 or 20 keywords that AdWords offers you by these criteria and working them into your campaign, with additional ads and other changes as needed. Tweak your campaign through weekly reviews, and then do a more systematic review after a month. Use that opportunity to run the tool again, and repeat the process.

> TIP: **Try Opportunities Monthly**
>
> At this writing, AdWords refreshes the information available through the Opportunities tab every few weeks. So, consider making a check of this tab part of a monthly routine for reviewing your AdWords account and its effectiveness. A monthly check might be a good opportunity for some deep thinking about how to get the most out of your account, with the Opportunities tab giving you food for thought.

Follow these steps to get ideas for your campaigns:

1. Within AdWords, click the **Opportunities** tab.

   The Ideas: All Online Campaigns page appears.

2. From the pull-down menu, choose each of the three options that are available, in turn: **Increase Traffic**, **Balance Cost and Traffic**, or **Maintain or Decrease Cost**. Note the number of keywords and the estimated monthly searches for each option.

   If the number of keywords and the estimated monthly searches are the same for two options, or all three, the suggestions are probably the same for those options. If AdWords has no suggestions for an option, it displays a generic list of recommendations for your campaign. (When I tried this, AdWords had no ideas for the Maintain or Decrease Cost option.)

   If the options have different numbers of keywords and estimated monthly searches, consider looking at all the options that are different.

3. Choose the option that looks most promising for your situation, balancing your desire for more clicks for your campaign against your tolerance for increased costs.

4. Click the **New Keywords For** link.

   A list of keywords appears, as shown in Figure 15.1. It includes the suggested keyword, the estimated monthly searches, a bar chart for the estimated strength of competition, and the ad group for which the keyword is recommended.

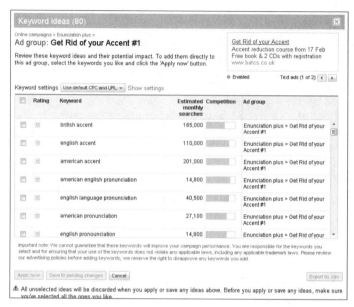

FIGURE 15.1   AdWords suggests keywords for you to evaluate and try.

The ad group shown is the one that the keyword is added to if you so choose, as described in the next few steps.

5. Consider the meaning of each suggested keyword against your products/services. Also review the estimated monthly services and the competition, and the performance of similar keywords in your existing campaign. With these factors in mind, click the check box next to each keyword that you want to keep.

6. To save your work on an interim basis, click the **Save to Pending Changes** button. When you're ready to implement the changes, and add all selected keywords to your account, click the **Apply Now** button.

The selected keywords are added to your account.

What happens now that you've added the selected keywords? The new keywords compete with existing keywords within your budget. You can then review your account regularly to prioritize the best keywords, add new ads that match up well against your best keywords to optimize click-throughs, improve your landing pages to support increased conversion, and generally improve your keywords. If results justify it, you might also consider increasing your AdWords budget.

You can revisit the Opportunities tab during a regularly scheduled checkup of your account, perhaps on a monthly basis. When you do so, you might see the same suggestions again and again. It takes "outside the box" thinking to come up with truly new keyword ideas. Use words and phrases that competitors use, that customers and vendors mention to you, and other sources, too, to get new ideas. AdWords then uses this new input to come up with its own suggestions.

All of this might seem like a lot of work, and potentially for little benefit. However, you can hit on new keywords that can be very helpful, as can the ongoing process of optimization I'm recommending here. For example, the strongest set of keywords for BATCS, "elocution" and variations on it, is neither obvious nor included in the BATCS website or other marketing materials. So, the process can prove quite useful.

NOTE: **Best Practices**

If AdWords doesn't have specific ideas for one or more of the options in the Opportunities tab, it offers a generic list of best practices instead. These recommendations are good to keep in mind for improving the effectiveness of your campaign. They include organizing your campaign around specific products, services, and so on; choosing your keywords carefully; including keywords in your ad text; matching destination URLs to specific ads; and tracking your success, as described in this lesson.

Improving Your Landing Pages

When you're on a path to optimizing your keywords, it's smart to start improving your landing page or pages within your website. At first, you should just link to pages you already have on your site that match the specific products or services you're advertising. Then you should consider specialized landing pages to support specific offers and the use of specific keywords.

There's a difference between Google's definition of success within AdWords and yours. For Google, a successful ad is one that gets lots of clicks because clicks mean you pay Google money. Google places your ad more frequently, and in higher positions, if it gets more clicks, even if your keyword bid is less. That's because your total payout to Google is higher than your competitors'.

For you, though, AdWords success is making lots of money from your Google ads. And it really should be lots of money; your AdWords payments come straight out of profits, and no one's paying you for the time you spend learning and using AdWords. So, your AdWords advertising really needs to pay off if it's going to be a good overall investment.

There are two keys to AdWords success:

▶ Getting clicks on your ads

▶ Converting those clicks into profitable sales

You can do all sorts of things to get your AdWords campaign going: spend lots of time on keywords, run specials that you lose a bit of money on, and more. However, eventually you need to create a program that runs a healthy profit without much further work on your part.

Your landing page is a huge part of this conversion process. Your landing page is, of course, the page that users see when they click your ad. An example of a simple landing page—a home page that's been adapted for use with AdWords—is shown in Figure 15.2.

The change shown in Figure 15.2 is quite simple. It supports ads for either the book that BATCS sells, *Get Rid of Your Accent*, or the in-person course. As BATCS gets more experience with what works and what doesn't, it can develop separate landing pages for the two offerings, special offers, and other innovations to support greater click-through and more conversions.

You can usefully encourage users to take three main types of actions after they arrive at your landing page:

▶ **Completing a purchase online.** This is the easiest thing to do psychologically for users because they don't need to switch modes. They can just keep clicking until they've finished with the purchase. The wording about *Get Rid of Your Accent* shown in Figure 15.2 supports an online purchasing process.

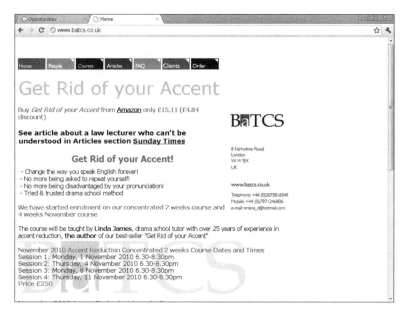

FIGURE 15.2 BATCS uses a modified home page as its AdWords landing page.

▶ **Calling you.** This can also be fairly easy for users, but only if they can call you immediately. If you're not available at the time that the user wants to act—this means, in most cases, that it's a time outside of business hours—chances are high that the user won't follow through, and you'll lose the sale. The details about online classes shown in Figure 15.2 support having the user make a call—the phone number for BATCS is on every page.

▶ **Visiting you.** This is the hardest thing to get users to do because it requires them to get up and move themselves, often by some kind of transportation, and usually after a delay. You're moving from an immediate, "act now" priority to just another item on the user's to-do list. In the case of BATCS, customers have to visit to take the class, but they're encouraged to call first rather than having to visit right away.

There are three dimensions to getting the user to act. The first is continuity on the computer, the second is immediacy in time, and the third is immediacy in space. Table 15.1 sums up the advantages and disadvantages of each method of completing a sale that begins with a click on your AdWords ad.

TABLE 15.1   The Advantages of AdWords Depend on How You Complete the Sale

	On Computer?	Immediate in Time?	Immediate in Location?
Online Purchase	Yes	Yes	Yes
Phone purchase	No	Sometimes	Yes
In-person purchase	No	No	No

TIP: **Repeating Keywords**

Just as Google recommends that you use the keyword that the user searched on in the ad that appears against that keyword, consider also doing the same with your landing page. Either include several of the keywords you use in each landing page, or consider going whole hog and revising your landing pages so that they're more or less specific for each keyword that you use, repeating it several times.

Considering that there's a specific cost per click for AdWords, and looking carefully at the plusses and minuses of different types of sales conversions, leads to some general recommendations:

▶ **Don't use AdWords for branding.** Using AdWords to get people to notice you, without a clear path to completing a sale, and tracking the completion, is likely to be a losing strategy. (You can fall into the trap represented by the old saying, "I know half my advertising spending is wasted; I just don't know which half.")

▶ **Use AdWords for online sales.** AdWords works well for driving online sales. Unfortunately, the online world is price competitive, so you have to sharpen your pencil to maintain profitability for the whole process. But AdWords is likely to be a good way to get customers in the (online) door.

▶ **Use AdWords for phone purchases during business hours.** AdWords also works well for phone sales, but much better if the call can be completed immediately. Geographic targeting might be a good practice for phone sales as well. Running your ad locally, and only during business hours—perhaps with some kind of "call now" exhortation—might be your best strategy.

▶ **Test AdWords and in-person sales carefully.** The attainment of *o2o sales* (online to offline; that is, moving the customer from an online impression to visiting your shop, store, or office) is actually quite powerful, but with lots of opportunity for the customer to drop out. Try this with tightly focused geographic targeting and track results carefully to make sure you really are generating profitable new business for your AdWords expenditures.

None of these recommendations is set in stone, by any means. However, they're good guidelines for initial AdWords investments. Start with an AdWords plan that takes these recommendations into account, carefully tracking spending and success. Then expand the parts of your investment that are winners, try new things, and cut back on unprofitable products, services, and sales approaches. This way, you can go from strength to strength, keep any losses to a minimum, and gradually identify all the ways that AdWords can be a winner for you.

Your landing page is the secret to making all these techniques work. It can be the first step in an online sale, part of an effort to get the user to call you, or an encouragement to come visit your shop or other location. You need to provide some product or service information, of course, but remember that the main goal is to complete a transaction.

So, don't waste your potential customer's time or energy: Provide the minimum amount of information needed to move the user on from one step to the next. For phone calls or an in-person visit, you can provide a bit of business information, make some kind of special offer to help get the customer in the door, and then leave off.

You want to track conversions, both from one step to the next, and from clicks to sales. And then, after tracking is in place, you want to optimize each step, ensuring that your clicks turn into sales as often (and as profitably) as possible.

> TIP: **Further Improving Your Landing Page**
>
> The Web offers a great deal of advice on improving your landing page, with new information constantly appearing. Consider searching in Google on the keywords "adwords landing page" to find the latest advice.

Don't be surprised if you spend just as much time and effort optimizing your landing page and other steps in the sales process as you do your AdWords ad, keywords selection, and so on. You might find yourself improving the online sales portion of your website (or even painting the inside of your physical shop!) to improve your AdWords-based selling process. It's all part and parcel of successfully doing business today.

AdWords offers many tools for improving your results, described throughout the rest of this lesson. Always be sure to keep in mind, though, how you're planning to sell, and how you actually make money, so that you get the most out of AdWords and out of your business as a whole.

Summary

In this lesson, you learned how to use the Opportunities feature in AdWords to improve your keywords and get more clicks for your ads. You also learned how to improve the landing pages on your site to improve your conversion rate from clicks to actual sales.

LESSON 16

Using Additional Reports and Tools

In this lesson, you learn how to use additional reports and tools that AdWords makes available for you. You learn how to use the Change History tool in depth, including viewing different reporting periods and comparing different statistics, such as clicks and cost, against changes you've made in your AdWords account.

Using Additional Reports

The options in the upper half of the Reporting and Tools menu relate to reporting. They include the following:

- ▶ **Change History.** The My Change History page displays changes you've made to your account, including new ads, new keywords, changes to budget amounts, and more.

- ▶ **Conversions.** Google has taken on the job of helping you click online conversions. After you create a conversion, as Google calls it, you receive code to place on your website to automatically track specific user actions.

- ▶ **Google Analytics.** Google Analytics is a powerful tool that supports you in improving your website as a lead-generation and, if you choose, online-sales tool. AdWords enables you to link your AdWords account to your existing Google Analytics account or to a new account that you create from within AdWords.

- ▶ **Website Optimizer.** The Website Optimizer is a powerful tool for testing the content of your site. It helps you get direct feedback from site visitors, improve your site, and test different website content to see which is most effective. It works with Google Analytics.

The three tools offered for improving your site—the Conversions Tool, Google Analytics, and Website Optimizer—overlap somewhat. However, the latter two tools, Google Analytics and the Website Optimizer, both require that you have a Google Analytics account.

> NOTE: **Using Google Analytics**
> Google Analytics is a complex tool in its own right, and using it properly depends on your having relatively in-depth knowledge of your website or a good working relationship with someone who does. It's probably more complicated than AdWords by itself. So, further information about Google Analytics isn't provided in this book. If you want to use Google Analytics, consider *Sams Teach Yourself Google Analytics in 10 Minutes* by Michael Miller (Sams, 2010).

This book covers only the Change History tool in detail because the Conversions Tool requires you to be able to insert code into your website—a somewhat technical exercise that varies greatly in its specifics, depending on how your site is set up. In addition, the Google Analytics tool and the Website Optimizer require you to have a Google Analytics account, which is a separate Google service.

Checking Your Account's Change History

The Change History tool is useful for keeping track of what you've done within your account. It tracks new ads, new keywords, changes to your budget, and more. It even charts these events against changes in metrics such as impressions, clicks, costs, and others.

These capabilities are valuable, but don't necessarily tell the whole story. There can be changes in the external world, in your business, in your website, and in other aspects of your online presence that significantly affect your AdWords results. These aren't recorded in AdWords, and there's no way to record them for use in AdWords reports such as those provided by the Change History tool.

The Change History tool also can't track why you made specific changes. As with changes in the external world, your website, and so forth, you want to record this information so that you have a narrative to help guide future changes.

The Change History tool does work at the campaign level—but not the Ad Group level. If you have a lot going on in a campaign—sales for different products/services, or for different physical locations, for instance—the Change History tool can't separate them out.

> TIP: **Campaigns and Change History**
> To make the Change History tool more useful, consider making campaigns relatively small and narrowly focused. This improves the usefulness of reporting at the campaign level, which the AdWords Change History tool makes available.

Finally, the Change History tool can't display the business impact of your AdWords work—sales made, profitability, and so on. For online sales, you can get this information from Google Analytics or other means. For offline sales, you have to record it (to the extent that you can track business activity directly back to AdWords) and combine it with AdWords reports, such as Change History, to understand the business picture.

So, keep separate records of what you do in AdWords, why you do it, and the business results that ensue. Only by doing so can you make good longer-term decisions about your AdWords spending as an overall part of your business.

The Change History tool is, however, a useful tool for identifying direct relationships between AdWords changes and key metrics. The metrics you can display are grand totals across all your campaigns, including search ads and display ads.

The metrics you can choose are impressions, clicks, clickthrough rate, cost, and conversions—if you have conversion tracking on, as described later in this lesson.

Follow these steps to check your account's change history:

1. Within AdWords, click the **Reporting and Tools** tab. Choose **Change History**.

The page My Change History appears, as shown in Figure 16.1.

FIGURE 16.1   You can view the change history for your account.

2. Choose the date range for your report.

The earliest beginning date available is January 1, 2006. You can either enter the end date and how far to go back—1 week, 2 weeks, 1 month, 3 months, 6 months, or 2 years—or click the **Select Exact Date Range** link to enter specific starting and finishing dates.

TIP: **Choosing the Date Range**

After you produce your report, you can use the Zoom capability, described in step 9, to zoom in within a given overall period. This means you can choose a long report period, such as the entire history of your account, and still easily get a close-in view of a briefer time period.

3. Enter the level of your account to be affected.

   As you start to type, a drop-down menu displays the choices available. Options are a Specific Campaign; Account Only, for changes made at the account level; or All Changes, for changes affecting all campaigns.

4. Click to set the check boxes that reflect the types of change you want to display. The possibilities are as follows:

   ▶ **All.** For all changes

   ▶ **Ad.** For new or revised advertisements

   ▶ **Budget.** For changes to the overall budget

   ▶ **CPC.** For cost-per-click bidding changes

   ▶ **Distribution.** For changes to the use of the Search Network versus the Display Network versus Mobile and so on

   ▶ **Keyword.** For changes to your keywords

   ▶ **Status.** For pausing or unpausing, or deleting or undeleting, a campaign or an ad group

   ▶ **Targeting.** For changes to geo-targeting or language targeting.

5. If you have multiple users on your account, use the drop-down menu in the Made By section to choose the user whose changes you want to see. The possibilities are as follows:

   ▶ **All.** For all changes

- ▶ **Ad.** For new or revised advertisements

- ▶ **Budget.** For changes to the overall budget

- ▶ **CPC.** For cost-per-click bidding changes

- ▶ **Distribution.** For changes to the use of the Search Network versus the Display Network versus Mobile and so on

- ▶ **Keyword.** For changes to your keywords

- ▶ **Status.** For pausing or unpausing, or deleting or undeleting, a campaign or an ad group

- ▶ **Targeting.** For changes to geo-targeting or language targeting.

6. Click the **Filter Change History** button.

   The report matching the changes you've made appears.

7. If needed, click the **Chart View** link to see the information as a graph, as in Figure 16.2.

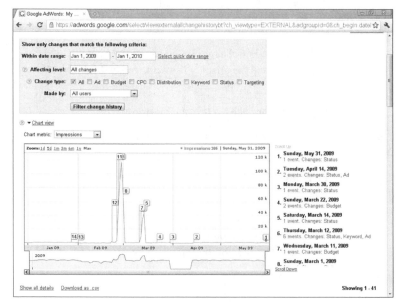

FIGURE 16.2   Change history charts match changes to metrics.

8. In Chart View, use the pull-down menu to switch among various metrics: Impressions, Clicks, Clickthrough Rate, Cost, or Conversions.

   The chart updates to reflect the chosen metric. Number indicators on the graphical chart reflect specific sets of changes to your account, which are referred to as *events*.

9. To set a zoom level, click one of the links, which may include the following:

   ▶ **1d.** For 1 day

   ▶ **5d.** For 5 days

   ▶ **1m.** For 1 month

   ▶ **6m.** For 6 months

   ▶ **1y.** For 1 year

   ▶ **Max.** For the entire period.

   Then drag the scroll arrows and scrollbar at the bottom of the chart to focus in on different parts of the overall period; drag the edges of the scroll box to change the period.

   The chart updates to reflect the choices you make.

10. Mouse over the chart to see the measurement of your chosen chart metric for a specific date.

11. View the table, as shown in Figure 16.3, to see specific changes to the account.

   A description of each change, including the date, user, campaign, ad group, and type of change, appears.

12. Under the Description heading, click the **Show** link to show the details for a specific change. Click the **Hide** link to hide the details.

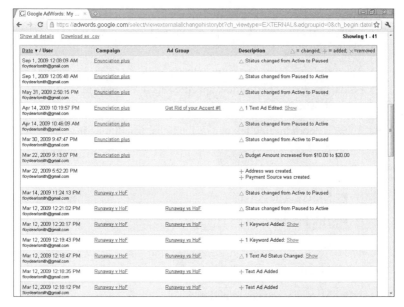

FIGURE 16.3   You can see all the changes you've made in a useful table.

13. For the table as a whole, click the **Show All Details** link to show details of the description of specific changes. To hide the details again, click the **Hide All Details** link.

The table expands to show all details or contracts to hide all details.

14. Click the **Download as .csv** link to export the change history. To save the file, choose a filename and download location and click **Save**.

The file is saved to your computer. You can open it in a spread-sheet program to edit it further.

Using Google Tools

Google offers a number of additional tools for use with your AdWords account. Some are available on the bottom half of the Reporting and Tools menu. Others are available via the More Tools link at the bottom of the menu.

Here are the tools available directly from the menu, shown in Figure 16.1:

► **Keyword Tool.** This tool helps you generate new keywords beginning with a word or phrase, or the URL of your website or a different website (perhaps a competing one). You can also set location or language to focus on, whether to include adult ideas or mobile search stats, whether to show results that don't include your original search terms, and filters for one or more specified criteria.

► **Traffic Estimator.** Get estimates for the traffic generated for specific keywords.

► **Placement Tool.** The Placement Tool is similar to the Keyword Tool, but it generates websites that might work well for a specific word, phrase, or words and phrases culled from a website that you specify.

► **Ads Diagnostic Tool.** Helps you see whether your ads are showing for a particular search.

► **Ad Preview Tool.** Preview your ad without generating actual impressions, which can mess up your stats (for the Search Network) or even cost you money (for the Display Network).

To see additional tools—potentially including new tools that have been added since this was written—click the **More Tools** link at the bottom of the Reporting and Tools menu. A page displaying available tools, as shown in Figure 16.4, appears.

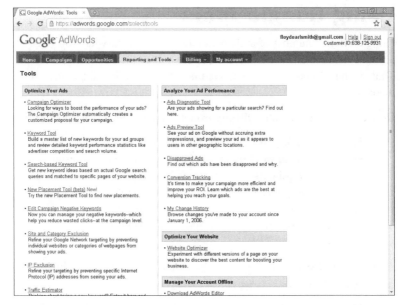

FIGURE 16.4   Google keeps coming up with new tools that you can use with AdWords.

Summary

In this lesson, you learned how to use additional reports and tools that AdWords makes available for you. You learned how to use the Change History tool in depth, including viewing different reporting periods and comparing different statistics, such as clicks and cost, against changes you've made in your AdWords account.

Index

J-K

L

M

Sams**TeachYourself**

from Sams Publishing

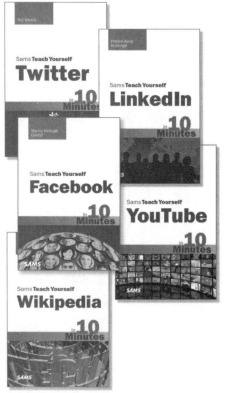

Sams Teach Yourself in 10 Minutes
offers straightforward, practical answers
for fast results.

These small books of 250 pages or less
offer tips that point out shortcuts and
solutions, cautions that help you avoid
common pitfalls, notes that explain
additional concepts, and provide additional
information. By working through the
10-minute lessons, you learn everything
you need to know quickly and easily!

When you only have time for the answers,
Sams Teach Yourself books are your
best solution.

Visit **informit.com/samsteachyourself**
for a complete listing of the products
available.

inform IT.com THE TRUSTED TECHNOLOGY LEARNING SOURCE

PEARSON

InformIT is a brand of Pearson and the online presence for the world's leading technology publishers. It's your source for reliable and qualified content and knowledge, providing access to the top brands, authors, and contributors from the tech community.

✦Addison-Wesley **Cisco Press** EXAM/**CRAM** **IBM** Press. QUE ‡‡ PRENTICE HALL S**A**MS | Safari

LearnIT at InformIT

Looking for a book, eBook, or training video on a new technology? Seeking timely and relevant information and tutorials? Looking for expert opinions, advice, and tips? **InformIT has the solution.**

- Learn about new releases and special promotions by subscribing to a wide variety of newsletters. Visit **informit.com/newsletters**.

- Access FREE podcasts from experts at **informit.com/podcasts**.

- Read the latest author articles and sample chapters at **informit.com/articles**.

- Access thousands of books and videos in the Safari Books Online digital library at **safari.informit.com**.

- Get tips from expert blogs at **informit.com/blogs**.

Visit **informit.com/learn** to discover all the ways you can access the hottest technology content.

Are You Part of the **IT** Crowd?

Connect with Pearson authors and editors via RSS feeds, Facebook, Twitter, YouTube, and more! Visit **informit.com/socialconnect**.

inform IT.com THE TRUSTED TECHNOLOGY LEARNING SOURCE   **PEARSON**

✦Addison-Wesley **Cisco Press** EXAM/**CRAM** **IBM** Press. QUE ‡‡ PRENTICE HALL S**A**MS | Safari

FREE Online Edition

Your purchase of **Sams Teach Yourself Google AdWords™ in 10 Minutes** includes access to a free online edition for 45 days through the Safari Books Online subscription service. Nearly every Sams book is available online through Safari Books Online, along with more than 5,000 other technical books and videos from publishers such as Addison-Wesley Professional, Cisco Press, Exam Cram, IBM Press, O'Reilly, Prentice Hall, and Que.

SAFARI BOOKS ONLINE allows you to search for a specific answer, cut and paste code, download chapters, and stay current with emerging technologies.

Activate your FREE Online Edition at www.informit.com/safarifree

> **STEP 1:** Enter the coupon code: RFMKYFA.

> **STEP 2:** New Safari users, complete the brief registration form. Safari subscribers, just log in.

If you have difficulty registering on Safari or accessing the online edition, please e-mail customer-service@safaribooksonline.com